New Ways in Teaching Vocabulary

Averil Coxhead, Editor

New Ways in TESOL Series

Innovative Classroom Techniques

TESOL International Association

Typeset in Aldine 401 and Humanist 777
by Capitol Communications, LLC, Crofton, Maryland USA
and printed by Gasch Printing, LLC, Odenton, Maryland USA

TESOL International Association
1925 Ballenger Avenue, Alexandria, Virginia 22314 USA
www.tesol.org

Publishing Manager: Carol Edwards
Cover Design: Citrine Sky Designs
Copyeditor: Sarah J. Duffy

TESOL Book Publications Committee
    John I. Liontas, Chair
    Robyn L. Brinks Lockwood, Co-chair
    Deoksoon Kim
    Jennifer Lebedev
    Adrian Wurr
    Gilda Martinez-Alba
    Guofang Li
    Project reviewers: Robyn L. Brinks Lockwood and Gail Schafers

ISBN 9781942223009
Library of Congress Catalogue No. 2014951674

Contents

Part I: Learning New Words and Phrases

Raising Awareness

Making Connections Between Words

Focusing on Multiword Units

Part II: Consolidating Vocabulary Learning

Consolidating Meaning

Consolidating Form

Working on Meaning and Form

Part III: Vocabulary and the Four Strands

Part IV: Strategies for Vocabulary Learning

Using Dictionaries

Learning More About Words

Developing Autonomy

Part V: Vocabulary and Technology

Finding Out More About Words

Words and Phrases in Context

Revising Vocabulary Using Technology

Part VI: Vocabulary for Specific Purposes

Making Decisions on Specialized Vocabulary

Using Specialized Vocabulary

INTRODUCTION

The purpose of this volume is to bring together a wide range of vocabulary-focused activities for language teachers. These activities can be used as they are or adapted to fit particular classrooms, learners, proficiency levels, technology, or needs. Each submission is categorized into a particular part and then into a subsection so that teachers can see where these ideas might fit into a wider program of vocabulary studies for their students. It would be a good idea to dip into different areas for activities to see how they might be adapted.

This revised volume of *New Ways in Teaching Vocabulary* is part of an ongoing strong interest in vocabulary studies in second and foreign language learning contexts. Its predecessor was edited by Emeritus Professor Paul Nation, Victoria University of Wellington, New Zealand. This new volume is timely, as vocabulary studies is an area of major growth over the last few decades. This growth has been supported and encouraged by Paul as one of the leading researchers and teachers in the field and his work is evident in the present volume in several ways. For example, Part III focuses on Nation's (2007, 2014) *four strands*: meaning-focused output, meaning-focused input, language-focused instruction, and fluency. The four strands concept suggests a way to organize and evaluate vocabulary learning in classroom activities, a vocabulary curriculum, and materials design. For more on ways in which he has influenced vocabulary studies, see Coxhead (2010).

The 1994 and current editions of this book are similar in that they both contain more than 90 teaching ideas focused on vocabulary in teaching and learning. These ideas represent a wide range of practical, well-tried, and practiced vocabulary activities. Both volumes begin with sections on learning new words and phrases and then move on to ways to develop deeper understanding of vocabulary. Some categories, such as strategies, collocation work, and encouraging autonomy, are represented in both volumes.

In many ways, however, this new volume is substantially different from the first edition. This revised volume was reconceptualized from the 1994 edition and all the submissions are new. Several new categories reflect developments in vocabulary studies. Vocabulary and Technology (Part V) was added because of the ever-growing use of technology in classrooms and their fairly easy connection with vocabulary studies. See Tom Cobb's (n.d.) website, the Compleat Lexical Tutor, for an example of how technology can adapt a range of vocabulary research and teaching ideas. We are lucky to have some submissions in the technology section from Tom in which he demonstrates the value and ease of using some of those tools. Vocabulary for Specific Purposes (Part VI) was added because of the international rise in language courses focused on preparing students for academic studies as well as for professional purposes.

In this new edition, there is also a wider focus on multiword units, particularly in Part I: Learning New Words and Phrases and Part IV: Strategies for Vocabulary Learning. Multiword unit research is burgeoning in vocabulary studies as we try to find out more about words as they appear in various combinations with other words in common collocations (for example, *bottom-up* and *data analysis*), phrases (for example, formulaic sequences; see Schmitt, 2010, for more on these sequences), lexical bundles, and so on.

Note that receptive and productive vocabulary activities are integrated in this volume. This book is organized into six parts. Part I focuses on learning new words and phrases, including presenting new words, developing connections in meaning, and concentrating on multiword units. Part II looks at consolidating knowledge of vocabulary in terms of meaning and form, and organizing learning. Part III draws on Nation's four strands. Part IV presents strategies for vocabulary learning, including dictionary training, practice, and developing autonomy. Part V is on vocabulary and technology, including ways to find out more about words, focus on them in context, and revise them. Last but not least, Part VI focuses on selecting lexical items to teach and ways to encourage learners to use specialized vocabulary.

Vocabulary is important in teaching and learning a language. In some ways, it is a central building block for all learners. It is unlikely that any language learner ever wished he or she had a smaller vocabulary. There is always room in any busy curriculum for good ideas to share. The contributors in this volume are all or have been teachers and are keen for you to try their ideas and adapt them to your learners, contexts, and needs. We hope you find many thoughtful, interesting, and useful vocabulary activities in this book.

I would very much like to acknowledge the creativity of the authors who submitted activities for this edition of *New Ways in Teaching Vocabulary*. Thank you also to TESOL Press for the editorial support, quick decision making, and guidance. Any errors or omissions are mine.

Averil Coxhead, Editor

REFERENCES

Cobb, T. (n.d.). *Compleat Lexical Tutor*. Retrieved from http://www.lextutor.ca

Coxhead, A. (Ed.). (2010). Special issue in honour of Paul Nation. *Reading in a Foreign Language, 22*(1).

Nation, I. S. P. (2013). *Learning vocabulary in another language* (2nd ed.). Cambridge, England: Cambridge University Press.

Nation, P. (2007). The four strands. *Innovation in Language Learning and Teaching, 11,* 2–13.

Schmitt, N. (2010). *Researching vocabulary*. Basingstoke, England: Palgrave Macmillan.

USER'S GUIDE TO ACTIVITIES

Each activity in this book starts with the suggested proficiency level of the learners that it is most appropriate for, followed by a short description of the aims of the activity. The time needed in class and for preparation is noted, along with a list of the resources that teachers will need. A step-by-step procedure is included for each activity, as well as suggestions for adaptation or other options. Any caveats or aspects of the activity that require consideration are also included.

Learning New Words and Phrases

- **Raising Awareness**
- **Making Connections Between Words**
- **Focusing on Multiword Units**

Part I: Learning New Words and Phrases

It is vitally important for learners to build a large vocabulary in the language they are studying. One way to approach the issue of how many words learners need to know is to find out how many and what kinds of vocabulary are in the texts that learners read. Various researchers have looked into the number of word families in different texts to see how big that vocabulary might need to be. A general rule of thumb for deciding how many words learners need in order to read a text without support is 98%, and with support is 95%. Different kinds of texts have different vocabulary loads. For example, Nation (2006) found that 98% is reached for newspapers, novels, and university-level texts at 8,000–9,000 word families plus proper nouns. Coxhead (2012) found the same load of 8,000–9,000 plus proper nouns at 98% coverage for novels that might be read at the secondary school level, such as *The Hunger Games* by Suzanne Collins and *Pride and Prejudice* by Jane Austen.

Studies have also looked at spoken language and vocabulary load. A study of movies by Webb & Rodgers (2009), for example, found 95% coverage was reached at 3,000 word families plus proper nouns and marginal words (such as fillers). The authors also found that 98% was reached at 6,000 word families plus proper nouns and marginal words. Dang and Webb (2014) looked at academic spoken English and found just over 96% coverage with 4,000 word families plus proper nouns, but 98% coverage at 8,000 word families plus proper nouns and marginal words. In another study, Coxhead and Walls (2012) developed a corpus of TED Talks (www.ted.com) and found that 95% was reached at 5,000 plus proper nouns, and 8,000–9,000 word families plus proper nouns were needed to reach 98%. Their finding suggests that TED Talks are closer in nature to academic writing. Studies like these can help us understand the vocabulary load of the texts we might be placing in front of students. You can find out how many words learners know or can recognize using Nation's Vocabulary Size Test (see Nation & Beglar, 2007). You can find a copy of the test on Tom Cobb's website, the Compleat Lexical Tutor (www.lextutor.ca).

Teachers and learners need to make clear decisions about which words they will focus on. They can make these decisions by looking at the frequency of words, for example, by concentrating on the most frequent words in the language they are learning (for more on frequency in vocabulary, see Nation, 2013; for a new General Service List of the most frequent words in English, see Brezina & Gablasova, 2013). Teachers and learners can make decisions about words to focus on by considering the goals for study. If learners are studying English for academic purposes, teachers might take into account word lists for their specialized subject area or general academic word lists such as the Academic Word List (Coxhead, 2000). Teachers might decide to concentrate on vocabulary items that learners already know something about (e.g., meaning, spelling) and focus on other aspects of the word that are not so well established (e.g., common collocations, limitations of use). Another way to select words is to consider the items that occur in classroom texts and whether learning them is important for language learning in general, for everyday use, for class, or for another important reason.

The activities in this section all in some way work on learners' encountering and focusing on learning new words and multiword units. Learners are encouraged to pay attention to aspects of word knowledge through a range of mostly interactive activities. This section also introduces working with multiword units, such as common collocations and phrases. Raising awareness of vocabulary in use is an important task for teachers.

REFERENCES

Brezina, V., & Gablasova, D. (2013). Is there a core general vocabulary? Introducing the new general service list. *Applied Linguistics.* Advanced online publication. doi:10.1093/applin/amt018

Coxhead, A. (2000). A new academic word list. *TESOL Quarterly, 34,* 213–238. doi:10.2307/3587951

Coxhead, A. (2012). Researching vocabulary in secondary school English texts: "The Hunger Games" and more. *English in Aotearoa, 78,* 34–41.

Coxhead, A., & Walls, R. (2012). TED Talks, vocabulary, and listening for EAP. *TESOLANZ Journal, 20,* 55–67.

Dang, T., & Webb, S. (2014). The lexical profile of academic spoken English. *English for Specific Purposes, 33,* 66–76. doi:10.1016/j.esp.2013.08.001

Nation, I. S. P. (2006). How large a vocabulary is needed for reading and listening? *Canadian Modern Language Review, 63*(1), 59–82. doi:10.3138/cmlr.63.1.59

Nation, I. S. P. (2013). *Learning vocabulary in another language,* 2nd ed. Cambridge, England: Cambridge University Press.

Nation, P., & Beglar, D. (2007). A vocabulary size test. *The Language Teacher, 31*(7), 9–13.

Webb, S., & Rodgers, M. P. H. (2009). The lexical coverage of movies. *Applied Linguistics, 30*(3), 407–427. doi:10.1093/applin/amp010

Word of the Day Presentation

Anne Jund and Kelly Kennedy

Levels	*All*
Aims	*Teach one word in depth to the class*
Class Time	*10 minutes per presentation*
Preparation Time	*35 minutes*
Resources	*Word of the Day planning tool for each student (Appendix A)*

Depending on resources, students may use poster paper and markers, chalk/ marker board, transparency paper and pens, overhead projector, PowerPoint slideshows (as in Appendix A), or online infographic generators (e.g., http://infogr .am, http://piktochart.com).

PROCEDURE

1. Explain that Word of the Day is a project to build English vocabulary by exploring many different aspects of one word each class day.

2. Model the first Word of the Day for students so that they understand the expectations for the activity.

3. Encourage students to utilize diverse contexts as potentially rich sources of interesting and challenging words, such as textbooks, novels, songs, movies, famous quotes, cartoons, video games, and other classmates' writing.

   a. Show students how to access academic word lists, corpuses, and ESL-friendly dictionaries on websites such as Wiktionary (www.wiktionary .org), ESL Desk (www.esldesk.com/vocabulary/academic), and Merriam Webster's Learner's Dictionary (www.learnersdictionary.com).

   b. Remind students to consider their audience of classmates and to choose a word that is likely unknown to others in order to maximize learning for everyone.

4. Provide students with a planning tool in the form of a list of questions about their word.

   a. What is the word? How do you spell it?

   b. How do you pronounce the word?

   c. Where did you read or hear the word?

   d. What is the part of speech of the word?

   e. What are the parts of the word (prefix, root word, suffix), if any?

   f. What is the meaning of the word in the context where you found it?

   g. Give a clear and easy-to-understand definition of the word.

   h. What are other possible meanings of the word?

   i. What other words are in the same word family?

   j. Give two or three example sentences that show how the word and other words in the family are used.

   k. What are synonyms and antonyms of the word, if any?

   l. How does the word translate into other languages (your own or your classmates' languages)?

   m. Share a picture, photograph, story, mnemonic device, or any other creative way to understand and remember the word.

   n. Write one discussion question that uses the word for your classmates to respond to.

5. Determine a schedule for the Word of the Day, using a sign-up sheet or other method.

6. Ask students to complete their planning tool and consult with you before their presentation.

7. Dedicate time during each class for students' Word of the Day presentations. Ask audience members to take notes during the presentation. Facilitate questions and discussions that arise, and support any additional meanings or understandings that may emerge.

8. Use a rubric (see Appendix B) to evaluate work and give feedback.

CAVEATS AND OPTIONS

1. Setting aside class time on a weekly (Word of the Week) basis works well.

2. Consider giving students the option to work in pairs to increase interaction and negotiation for meaning. This option may be especially practical in large classes.

3. Choose fewer questions to shorten the activity.

4. Include additional assessments such as a culminating vocabulary quiz, game, or writing project that uses all Words of the Day.

5. Consider publishing and sharing students' Words of the Day on a class website or social media page.

REFERENCES AND FURTHER READING

Baker, E. A. (Ed.). (2010). *The new literacies: Multiple perspectives on research and practice*. New York, NY: Guildford Press.

Ebbers, S. (2009). *Vocabulogic*. Retrieved from http://vocablog-plc.blogspot.com

Lankshear, C., & Knobel, M. (Eds.). (2011). *New literacies everyday practices and social learning* (3rd ed.). Maidenhead, England: Open University Press.

APPENDIX A: *Teacher-Created Exemplar*

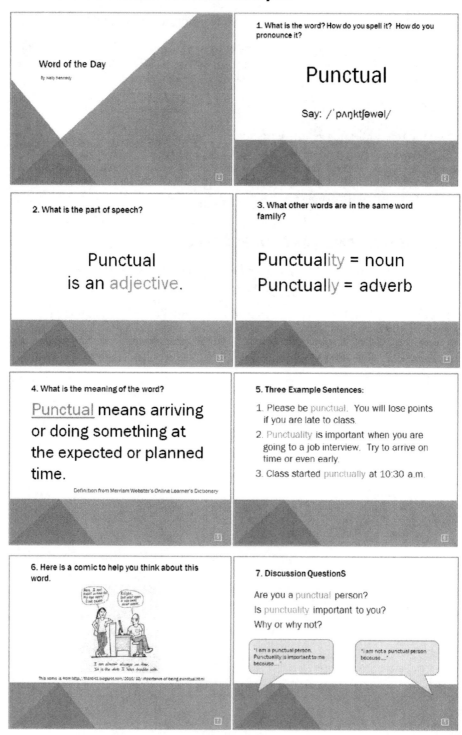

APPENDIX B: *Rubric*

	Word of the Day Presentation Evaluation	
	Criteria	**Points 0–2**
1	Your presentation was well planned and organized.	
2	You gave a clear definition of your word.	
3	You gave detailed information about your word.	
4	You gave good examples to show how the word is used.	
5	You shared a meaningful story, picture, or memory trick to help the class understand and remember the word.	
	TOTAL	_____/10 points

0 = missing/absent; 1 = needs improvement; 2 = good work

Interjections!

Mike Misner

Levels	**Intermediate +**
Aims	**Become familiar with many expressions that are rarely in dictionaries or textbooks but are frequently used in everyday conversation**
Class Time	**40 minutes**
Preparation Time	**5 minutes**
Resources	**PowerPoint presentation**
	Graphic organizer

PROCEDURE

1. Project or give a worksheet with several interjections and onomatopoeic phrases (e.g., *ack, wow, yikes, duh, huh, tsk tsk, whew, dang, hey, yo, shoot, uh-huh, unh-uh*), according to the needs of the students.

2. Have students listen and expressively repeat the pronunciations of each of the interjections after you do.

3. Encourage students to use online dictionaries and lists of interjections, as necessary, to discover the meanings and translations of any interjections that they do not already know.

4. Tell students to place the interjections in a graphic organizer that has categories such as *surprise, admiration, disappointment, disgust*, and so on (according to the needs of the students).

Surprise	Admiration	Disappointment	Disgust	Relief
yikes	wow	tsk tsk	ack	whew

5. Have students check their answers with their partners or in groups by reading the category and all of the interjections which fit that category.

6. If there is disagreement, the groups should refer to their online resources and discuss the disagreement until a consensus is reached.

7. Tell students to create a dialogue which incorporates the interjections that they just studied.

8. Have the small groups present their dialogues to each other. Several small groups should be presenting simultaneously in different corners of the room.

9. Tell students to switch groups and present again. Repeating the activity leads to greater organization, comprehension, and fluency.

CAVEATS AND OPTIONS

1. Students should not dismiss the content of this lesson as slang. Interjections may not frequently appear in texts or dictionaries, but they are often used across all registers and levels of proficiency, especially for telling and back-channeling to stories.

2. To exemplify Caveat 1, play a short video showing proficient English speakers correctly using several interjections while telling stories (e.g., the *School House Rock* version of the song introducing interjections: www.youtube.com/watch?v=_e24kdjdbtw).

3. There are several online lists of interjections with definitions such as the one at Daily Writing Tips: www.dailywritingtips.com/100-mostly-small-but-expressive-interjections.

4. Use emoticons or first language translations if the category terms at the top of the graphic organizer are too difficult for students.

5. Check any overlap between interjections in English and in students' first language, which will make teaching and learning this set of uncommonly taught vocabulary as easy as it is useful.

Greyish Blueish Green!

Marlise Horst and Joanna White

Levels	*Beginning, high-beginning*
Aims	*Increase awareness of the suffix* –ish
Class Time	*15–20 minutes*
Preparation Time	*5 minutes*
Resources	*Student copies or projection of Shel Silverstein's poem "Colors"*

PROCEDURE

1. Prepare copies or a projection of the poem "Colors," by Shel Silverstein (1974) that begins "My skin is kind of sort of brownish." It is widely available on the Internet.

2. Tell students to read the poem. Or you may want to read it aloud first before they see it. The reading (or listening) focus question is: What ending do you notice on the colour words? Answer: –*ish*.

3. Then ask about the meaning of –*ish*: What is the difference between *yellow* and *yellowish*? Answer: Yellowish is sort of yellow, not true yellow.

4. Students read the poem aloud to each other in pairs. Each partner may change two or three colour words to personalize the poem to his or her own colouring.

5. For students who finish early: What colours are not mentioned (in either the normal or –*ish* form)? Answer: purple, black (and possibly others). Point out that these can have –*ish* endings, too.

6. Before moving on, you may wish to ask students about the message of the poem. Does it have a message? Maybe it is just a silly poem, or maybe the author is saying that skin colour is impossible to describe and doesn't matter?

7. Point out that there are many other uses of –*ish*, including adjectives for nationalities. Students will know *English* and possibly others. Elicit these using this question frame:

What is the adjective for people from _____? (What is the adjective for people from England? Answer: English.)

Some countries that use this suffix are England, Spain, Turkey, Poland, Ireland, Scotland, Sweden, Denmark, and Finland.

CAVEATS AND OPTIONS

1. Here are some additional questions to ask using the frame: How do we describe a person who . . . ?

    acts like a <u>baby</u> all the time (*babyish*)

    spends all his or her time reading <u>books</u> (*bookish*)

    is an older woman but acts like a little <u>girl</u> (*girlish*)

    thinks about him<u>self</u> or her<u>self</u> only and never about others (*selfish*)

    likes to wear fashionable clothes and dress in <u>style</u> (*stylish*)

    acts like a <u>child</u> younger than his or her real age (*childish*)

2. Students may be interested to know that –*ish* is used creatively in English to make new words (e.g., "No thanks, I'm not feeling very *pizza-ish* today").

3. The suffix –*ish* is relatively easy for beginning learners to use in the sense that adding it does not usually change the spelling of the base word (unlike *ugly/uglier, fame/famous,* etc.).

REFERENCES AND FURTHER READING

Bauer, L., & Nation, P. (1993). Word families. *International Journal of Lexicography, 6,* 253–279. doi:10.1093/ijl/6.4.253

Schmitt, N., & Zimmerman, C. B. (2002). Derivative word forms: What do learners know? *TESOL Quarterly, 36,* 145–171. doi:10.2307/3588328

Silverstein, S. (1974). "Colors." In *Where the sidewalk ends.* New York, NY: Harper & Row.

Collaborative Conversations for Learning New Vocabulary

Haidee Thomson

Levels	*Intermediate to high*
Aims	*Expand experience using new vocabulary and phrases*
Class Time	*10 minutes*
Preparation Time	*None*
Resources	*Paper*
	Pens
	Whiteboard

This activity is good for small classes with a conversation focus. New words and phrases which emerge through group discussion are used generatively by learners in original texts and then peer reviewed and self-edited before being shared again with the group.

PROCEDURE

1. Encourage conversation between learners. This could mean each person shares what he or she did in the weekend or exchanges knowledge or opinions on chosen topics. You can participate in the conversation, but allow the learners to do most of the talking.

2. Provide scaffolding for words or phrases that learners search for or need help with to produce correctly as part of the conversation.

3. Write on a whiteboard any new or partially known words or phrases that emerge, so that a list of newly encountered or in-need-of-revision language develops. Having a visible reference on the whiteboard allows learners to easily reuse and experiment with this language in the course of the conversation.

4. To introduce the activity, take advantage of a natural break in the conversation once there are several words or phrases on the whiteboard.

5. Instruct learners to select one word or phrase from the list generated during the conversation that they want to practise.

6. Tell learners to write a sentence or short paragraph (depending on their level) using that word or phrase. Once they have finished, have them read it over to check for coherence.

7. Model swapping texts with a partner, reading your partner's text and underlining any sections that you think might need reviewing or correcting. Be careful to underline rather than correct. Return the text to the writer and receive your text back with your partner's underlining. Look at the underlined areas to decide how to improve the text in light of the indirect feedback.

8. Tell learners to swap texts and review their partner's text as you have modelled.

9. Instruct learners to show revised texts to you.

10. Underline any areas that were missed in peer review that still need review or correction.

11. Tell learners to make changes to the text if necessary in light of the feedback. You can also give more explicit feedback if there is need.

12. Ask learners to share (read/recite) their revised texts with the group.

13. Encourage the group to ask the speaker questions afterwards in relation to the content of their text. From here the activity can start again, if desired, from the follow-up discussion.

CAVEATS AND OPTIONS

1. Keep a close eye on the reviewing process. Learners should simply underline a problem which the original writer can then decide how to edit. They should not correct their partner's writing.

2. To increase the challenge, have learners recite their final sentences from memory, rather than read them.

Collective Gifting and Sharing of Vocabulary

Jannie van Hees

Levels	*Intermediate to advanced*
Aims	*Expand topic-related vocabulary knowledge*
	Deepen comprehension of shared vocabulary
Class Time	*20–30 minutes*
Preparation Time	*20–30 minutes*
Resources	*Approximately five topic-related visuals*
	One piece of paper per student and for the teacher
	Display board and data projector

PROCEDURE

1. Introduce the topic. In pairs, have students share their current knowledge and thinking about the topic by brainstorming ideas.

2. Show the class the topic-related visuals one at a time. Stimulate spontaneous responses by students about the visuals and their thinking.

3. Have individual students write down any words or word groups that come to mind while viewing visuals (about 5–10 minutes).

4. While they are working individually, record your own ideas for words or word groups on your piece of paper. You could include any vocabulary items that students are likely to write down, ones they may not think of or know, or words that are important topic-related vocabulary items.

5. Pair up the students again and have them share their list of words and word groups. Have students take turns calling out one word or word group on their sheet. Tell their partner to check to see whether they also wrote down this word or word group. If so, they tick it; if not, they add it to their list.

6. As each student nominates a word or word group, have him or her explain how he or she thinks each one is related to the topic. Have the student's partner add to this explanation or challenge its relatedness. By consensus, students should either retain or delete the item.

7. Get each pair to check for spelling accuracy.

8. Continue until all words and word groups are shared. Throughout, walk around the room to monitor process and gauge vocabulary range.

9. Working as a class, have students take turns to share one word or word group from their list and its relationship to the topic. Other students and you may add to this explanation or challenge its relatedness. Class consensus decides whether to retain or throw out the item.

10. For each nominated item, have students check to see if it is on their list. If it is, they underline it; if not, they add it to their list. Check for spelling accuracy.

11. As a final class exercise, share your vocabulary items by showing each word at a time. As before, have students check their list. If the words you are showing are on their lists, have them circle the words. If they are not on their lists, have them add the words to their lists.

12. Following each show and check, have students in pairs try to explain or challenge the relatedness of each word to the topic.

13. Students check for spelling accuracy.

14. Finally, as a class, encourage students to share ideas about the topic that they gained throughout the brainstorming process.

CAVEAT AND OPTIONS

1. A valuable next step is to move on to a mind-mapping task. Put students in pairs or small groups and ask them to sort and group the vocabulary on the final list. They could do this by cutting up their list, discussing possible ways of grouping and why, and creating headings under which to sort the vocabulary. Grouping and placement should be based on consensus, with each item thoroughly discussed. It should not simply become a sort-and-place exercise with minimal dialogue and meaning sharing. Carry out a group assessment as above.

2. The approach at this early stage of language learning is not recommended. If students are orally capable but struggle somewhat in writing, the approach still works. Students simply write down their words as best they can. Spelling accuracy is given attention along the way.

3. The approach can be used at the beginning of a topic or to establish key ideas along the way, or as a final stock-take and review.

4. Careful selection of visuals is important. They are key triggers to support students with little to no knowledge of the topic in hand.

REFERENCES AND FURTHER READING

Slavin, R. E. (1991). Synthesis of research on cooperative learning. *Educational Leadership, 48*(5), 71–82.

Vocabulary Comics

Jay Tanaka

Levels	*Intermediate +*
Aims	*Strengthen memory of new vocabulary*
Class Time	*10–15 minutes*
Preparation Time	*None*
Resource	*Notebook for each student*

Illustrations can provide an enjoyable way for students to learn new vocabulary. Vocabulary comics are example sentences complemented by simple sketches. This combination helps both student and the teacher confirm understanding of new words, phrases, and expressions. Giving students the opportunity to create their own original example sentences strengthens memory through generative processing (Nation, 2001). In addition, vocabulary comic entries are often fun and humorous, which can help develop positive attitudes toward vocabulary learning.

PROCEDURE

1. Ask students to search recent readings and textbook activities for newly discovered words, phrases, and expressions. Encourage them to select vocabulary that they find interesting and useful. It is also possible to have students prioritize learning of words that appear most commonly in English (high-frequency vocabulary). Academic vocabulary can also be a useful target for vocabulary comics. Any word can be used as long as it appears in a sentence that has an illustratable image.

2. At the top of a blank notebook page, have students write the sentence in which they discovered the new word.

3. Below the sentence, ask students to draw a quick sketch of the situation that the sentence describes. This process serves two purposes: It allows you to check students' understanding of the word in context, and it strengthens students' memory of the vocabulary in context.

4. Halfway down the same page, ask students to write their own original example sentence reusing the same word, phrase, or expression *in a different context*. Students should have the freedom to either replicate the same grammar pattern from the sentence at the top of the page or explore different parts of speech and/or definitions. The purpose of this is to support learner autonomy and the exploration of vocabulary. You should later check these original example sentences and offer feedback and encouragement.

5. Below the original example sentence, ask students to draw another quick sketch of the situation that the original example sentence describes. Sometimes usage errors can make the original sentence hard to understand for you. This second illustration makes it possible for you to confirm students' intended meaning in the sentence and makes it easier to provide feedback. Also, the act of thinking up and sketching the image strengthens students' memory of the vocabulary.

6. Repeat the process. Students use one word, phrase, or expression to write two sentences and draw two sketches per page. The end result is a comic book of illustrations and captions using new vocabulary, which you can check periodically and provide feedback within a reasonable amount of time.

CAVEATS AND OPTIONS

1. You can decide whether to set a requirement for number of entries. Depending on the situation, it may be useful to set a periodic requirement and/or a goal for number of entries.

2. It is important to steer students away from rarely occurring vocabulary that has limited use.

3. Students' original example sentences can sometimes be extremely short and nearly devoid of context. Encourage students to use the new vocabulary to create sentences that describe personal experiences. Explain that writing more will make the memory of the sentences stronger and clearer.

REFERENCES AND FURTHER READING

Laufer, B., & Hulstijn, J. (2001). Incidental vocabulary acquisition in a second language: The construct of task-induced involvement. *Applied Linguistics*, *22*(1), 1–26. doi:10.1093/applin/22.1.1

Nation, I. S. P. (2001). *Learning vocabulary in another language*. Cambridge, England: Cambridge University Press.

Stahl, S. A., & Fairbanks, M. M. (1986). The effects of vocabulary instruction: A model-based meta-analysis. *Review of Educational Research, 56*(1), 72–110.

Learning Word Stress Along With New Vocabulary

John Murphy

Levels	*All*
Aims	*Develop the habit of learning patterns of word stress for new vocabulary*
	Gain confidence in using new words
Class Time	*20 minutes*
Preparation Time	*Minimal*
Resources	*Relevant listening and reading texts*

Part of what it means to know a new word includes being able to use it as part of one's active vocabulary. To do so, students need to learn patterns of word stress for new words. This activity focuses learners' attention in this direction.

PROCEDURE

1. As often as is relevant, ask students to bring to class a list of 5–10 new words they have recently encountered through either reading or listening, words they'd like to be able to use in conversation. See the Appendix for some examples of words and common patterns of word stress.

2. Challenge students to figure how many syllables each word contains. As needed, teach what syllables are and how to count them.

3. If students don't know the number of syllables in a word, some options are to check syllable counts in the pronunciation key of a dictionary, listen carefully as a more proficient speaker pronounces the word, or try to figure it out on their own.

4. Tap out the number of syllables in a word. Demonstrate and ask students to use some sort of a physical gesture (e.g., counting on fingers; tapping on desktops) to develop a sensory feel for the number of syllables in a word.

5. Ask students which syllable is the strongest. Help them determine which of the word's syllables is its strongest (most clearly enunciated, loudest).

6. If students are unsure which syllable is strongest, repeat Step 3, or encourage them to make an educated guess by applying rules for word stress (see, e.g., Celce-Murcia, Brinton, Goodwin, & Griner, 2010, pp. 187–194).

7. Especially if it's a longer word, determine whether or not the word has another strong-ish syllable (i.e., secondary stressed).

8. Label the word's stress pattern with a numeric system. This is the most important step. To retain word stress information, and to have shared conventions for discussing word stress patterns in class, students label each new word with a numeric system (either two or three digits) as follows: The word *deTERmine* is a 3-2 word, meaning it's a three-syllable word with primary stress on its second syllable. The word **SYL***lable* is a 3-1 word (three syllables with primary stress on its first syllable). For longer words a three-digit system may apply. For example, *voCAbulary* may be described as either a 5-2 word (five syllables with primary stress on its second syllable) or a 5-2-1 word, whereby we acknowledge that its initial syllable also carries some secondary stress (i.e., *VOCAbulary*). Similarly, the word *PREPpaRAtion* is best described as a 4-3-1 word (four syllables, with primary stress on the third syllable and secondary stress on its first syllable).

9. Use additional forms of physical gestures. Once patterns of word stress have been established (and to render students' encounters with new words more memorable), involve students in coordinating physical gestures with patterns of word stress as they say their words aloud. Some alternative gestures include the following:

   - lightly tapping pencils on desktops
   - opening and closing hands like clam shells
   - using shoulder shrugs and/or raised eyebrows
   - while seated, lifting feet in synchrony with stressed syllables
   - practicing easy dance steps
   - playing hand games like "Pat-a-cake, Pat-a-cake"
   - walking around the room while coordinating footsteps

- sharing handshakes and high fives coordinated with the enunciation of primary stressed syllables

- placing one's index fingers inside the loop of a thick rubber band to facilitate stretching the band apart on the word's stressed syllables

CAVEATS AND OPTIONS

1. Restrict the words students select to those appearing, or featured, in course materials.

2. Leave word selection completely up to learners.

3. Teach, practice, and refer frequently to the numeric system in class.

REFERENCES AND FURTHER READING

Celce-Murcia, M., Brinton, D., Goodwin, J., & Griner, B. (2010). *Teaching pronunciation: A course book and reference guide* (2nd ed.). New York, NY: Cambridge University Press.

Murphy, J. M. (2004). Attending to word-stress while learning new vocabulary. *English for Specific Purposes, 23*(1), 67–83. doi:10.1016/S0889-4906(03)00019-x

Murphy, J. M. (2013). *Teaching pronunciation*. Alexandria, VA: TESOL.

Murphy, J. M., & Kandil, M. (2004). Word-level stress patterns in the academic word list. *System, 32*, 61–74. doi:10.1016/j.system.203.06.001

APPENDIX: *Common Patterns of Word Stress Arranged According to Frequency of Occurrence in the Academic Word List*

Pattern	Word
3-2	com**MIT**ment
2-2	app**ROACH**
4-2	com**PLEX**ity
2-1	**VER**sions
4-3-1	ECo**NOM**ic
3-1	**AN**alyst
4-1-3	**QUAL**iTAtive
3-1-3	**IN**stiTUTE
5-3-1	METHo**DOL**ogies
5-2-4	dis**CRI**miNATing
4-2-4	fa**CIL**iTATE
4-1	**VAR**iable
3-3-1	GUARan**TEE**
2-1-2	**NET**WORKS

Primary stress = bolded capital letters; secondary stress = capital letters only.

Teaching Vocabulary Using a Seasonal Weather Chart

Jolene Jaquays and Sara Okello

Levels	*Beginning*
Aims	*Use connection between vocabulary related to seasons*
	Put the vocabulary into context with the other associated words
	Review capitalization rules regarding seasons, months, and sentences
Class Time	*30–50 minutes*
Preparation Time	*5 minutes*
Resources	*Unlined paper*
	Colored paper
	Colored pencils or markers

Drawing pictures appeals to kinesthetic learners who like to move and visual learners who like to see images. This activity appeals to both types of learners and presents vocabulary in a meaningful, communicative context. (For more on learning styles and vocabulary learning, see Cunningham Florez & Burt, 2001; Tight, 2010; Yeh, Wang, & Tsing, 2003.)

PROCEDURE

1. Do this activity after students have been taught the vocabulary for seasons, weather, months of the year, sports, and basic activities. Students should also know simple present tense.

2. Provide a sheet of unlined paper to each student. Have colored paper and colored pencils or markers available.

3. Instruct students to divide their paper into four quarters.

4. Instruct students to label each quadrant one of the four seasons. Remind them that seasons are not capitalized. Continue to model.

5. For each season, have students write the three months that are associated with the season (in the United States). Remind them that months are capitalized. (This activity can be adapted for learners and teachers outside the United States by including the seasons in their country, e.g., dry, rainy.)

6. Tell students to write two weather expressions for each season. Encourage them to use eight weather expressions in total.

7. Instruct students to write two simple sentences in which they say what they like to do. Tell them one of the activities should be a sport associated with the season. If they don't like a sport of that season, they can write "I don't like to _____."

CAVEATS AND OPTIONS

1. This activity can also be done with magazine pictures if students do not want to draw.

2. In addition, students can do this activity on computers, in which case you may need to provide additional instruction on searching for and inserting graphics.

3. Once students finish making their weather charts, you can have them give a presentation to the class about their weather chart to combine the skills of listening and speaking with vocabulary.

4. You can also display the weather charts on the walls of your classroom.

5. As a follow-up activity, students can write a paragraph about their favorite season with the framework that has already been provided.

REFERENCES AND FURTHER READING

Cunningham Florez, M. A., & Burt, M. (2001). *Beginning to work with adult English language learners: Some considerations.* Retrieved from http://www.cal.org/caela/esl_resources/digests/beginQA.html

Tight, D. G. (2010). Perceptual learning style matching and L2 vocabulary acquisition. *Language Learning, 60,* 792–833. doi:10.1111/j.1467-9922.2010.00572.x

Yeh, Y., Wang, C. W., & Tsing, N. (2003). Effects of multimedia vocabulary annotations and learning styles on vocabulary learning. *Calico Journal, 21*(1), 131–144.

APPENDIX: *Sample Weather Chart*

winter
December
January
February

It's cold. I like to ski.
It snows. I like to drink hot chocolate.

spring
March
April
May

It's warm. I like to plant flowers.
It rains. I like to play baseball.

Cognate Shopping

Philippa Bell, Marlise Horst, and Joanna White

Levels	*High beginning to low intermediate*
Aims	*Develop skills in recognizing helpful cognate relationships*
Class Time	*15 minutes*
Preparation Time	*None*
Resources	*Blackboard and chalk*
	Pictures of food items

This alphabet shopping list activity is suited to classes in which the learners and the teacher have a first language in common.

PROCEDURE

1. Start by saying, "I went to market and I bought an apple." The next player then says, "I went to market and I bought an apple and a banana." Continue with food words on through the alphabet. Each player must repeat all of the previous items and add a new one.

2. When students can't go any further, ask the whole class to call out the list while you write each word on the board. Put cognates on one side and non-cognates on the other. Thus in the case of French-speaking learners of English, *apple* (= *pomme* in French) is on the non-cognate side, but *banana* (= *banane* in French) belongs on the cognate side. Don't explain the reason for the two lists (yet).

3. Ask students why you have written two separate lists. What is the difference between them? Elicit the idea that all the words on one list are the same or similar in the shared first language (i.e., cognates) whereas the others are not.

4. If you have any students who speak other languages, ask them if the list would be divided the same way in their languages. Sometimes even non-European languages have surprisingly similar food names. For example, in

(Mandarin) Chinese *coffee* is *kafei*, *tofu* is *doufu*, and *chocolate* is *chakeli*. Guide the discussion toward the conclusion that knowing other languages can be very helpful in learning English words.

CAVEATS AND OPTIONS

1. Food pictures or a picture dictionary may be useful as prompts if students get stuck on a letter.

2. To expand on the activity, have students work in teams to see which team can create the biggest shopping list using only words that are the same (or similar) in English and the class's shared language. They don't have to stick to food shopping.

3. Generally, cognates in concrete domains (food, sports, science, clothing, jobs, etc.) tend to be good friends. False friend problems often arise in using more abstract words.

4. The learners' first language may not lend itself to this activity. Friendly English cognates are widely available to learners who speak a European language, but they are far less available in other languages.

REFERENCES AND FURTHER READING

Granger, S. (1996). Romance words in English: From history to pedagogy. *KVHAA Konforenser, 36*, 105–121.

Horst, M., White, J., & Bell, P. (2010). First and second language knowledge in the language classroom. *International Journal of Bilingualism, 14*, 331–349. doi:10.1177/1367006910367848

White, J., & Horst, M. (2012). Cognate awareness-raising in late childhood: Teachable and useful. *Language Awareness, 21*, 181–196.

Semantic Gradient

Mike Misner

Levels	Beginner (young learners)
Aims	Learn about the concept of relationships between words
Class Time	10 minutes
Preparation Time	10 minutes
Resources	Set of word cards
	Paper or felt board to display the word cards

PROCEDURE

1. Prepare enough sets of word cards for all of the pairs in your class.

2. Possible sets include size words (e.g., *tiny, small, medium, large, huge, gigantic, enormous*), colors of the rainbow (e.g., *red, orange, yellow, green, blue, indigo, violet*), or times of day (e.g., *morning, afternoon, evening, night*).

3. Give a set of out-of-order word cards to each pair of students.

4. Have students discuss what the best order would be and place/display the words in the correct order on a paper or felt board. If there is disagreement, students should discuss the situation until there is consensus. (It is acceptable for students to negotiate meaning in their first language in this activity.)

5. When the correct order has been found, the order and the rationale for that order should be presented to another team or to the class.

CAVEATS AND OPTIONS

1. Give different sets of words to different pairs, and rotate all of the pairs through several semantic gradient activity stations.

2. Have the pairs choose their own words and make their own word cards to formulate their own semantic gradients according to their own rationales.

3. Use this technique for processes (e.g., the rain cycle, the life cycle of a butterfly, the growth of a tree from a seed).

4. Instead of a gradient, use this technique as a Venn diagram, semantic field, cause-effect, or other order.

Working With Collocations in Texts

Anna Siyanova-Chanturia

Levels	*Any*
Aims	*Identify and work with collocations*
	Gain awareness of collocations in texts
Class Time	*10–15 minutes per activity*
Preparation Time	*5–15 minutes*
Resources	*Texts that students read in class (or at home)*

PROCEDURE

1. Use a text from class that students have already read. Give them a set of verbs (perhaps approximately 10) and ask them to find the nouns that these verbs collocate with in the text.

2. Working as a whole class, ask students to create one new sentence with two of the collocations they found in the text to see if they can use them in new contexts. Write the class sentences on the board and have everyone check them for accuracy. Repeated practice will help learners with these collocation patterns.

3. Divide the class into two groups. Ask both groups to come up with new sentences using the verb-noun collocations from the text. Ask them to include only one collocation per sentence and to provide sufficient context, like they did as a whole class in Step 2. Check their sentences for accuracy.

4. Have students write out each sentence with a blank or gap in the place of the collocations on a new piece of paper. They are creating an activity for the other students in the class.

5. Ask the two groups to swap their sentences. Each group's task is to complete the sentences of the other group using the right collocation. Once the sentence completion task is done, ask the two groups to check each other's answers.

CAVEATS AND OPTIONS

1. The type of collocations to focus on will depend on the text that the students have read. Texts will vary greatly in the number and type of collocations that they contain. Be careful to select a manageable number to work with.

2. You can isolate the collocations from the text by creating a matching activity like the one below and ask students to put the verbs into the table next to the nouns to form the collocations used in the text. For example:

   a. lose (*control*)

   b. restore (*balance*)

   c. reach

   d. develop

   e. combat

   f. treat

   g. give

Verb	Noun
	blood
	peaks
	infections
	complications
	balance
	disorders
	boost

Another example of a matching activity would be to have students match one adjective in the left column below with one noun in the right column to create adjective + noun collocations which appear in a text that the students have already read.

allergic
overnight
extensive
medieval
wide
mental
commercial

express
variety
use
illness
trade
reaction
times

allergic ➔ *reaction*

overnight ➔ *express*

etc.

3. Ask students to find all noun + noun collocations in a text that they have already read. Then ask them to write them down and explain their meaning. For example: "*A telephone directory* is an alphabetic list of names and telephone numbers."

APPENDIX: *Common Types of Collocations*

Verb + noun collocations

> *combat terrorism*
>
> *restore peace*
>
> *lose control*

Some of the most common English verbs are *have, take, make, give,* and *do* (so-called delexical verbs). These verbs can be combined with many different nouns to form frequent verb + noun collocations.

Noun + noun collocations

These collocations are very common in English. In such collocations, the first noun defines the second. The second noun is called "head" noun. For example:

> *chocolate bar*: a bar of chocolate
>
> *school teacher*: a teacher at school
>
> *safety belt*: a belt to use for personal safety

Adjective + noun collocations

> *strong tea*
>
> *false accusations*
>
> *physical activity*

Collocation Instruction

Seonmin Park

Levels	*Intermediate*
Aims	*Learning collocations for authentic language use*
Class Time	*10 minutes*
Preparation Time	*2–3 minutes*

PROCEDURE

1. Ask students whether they know what a collocation is. Introduce a definition of a collocation (a way that words are combined with each other) and explain why they need to learn collocations (improving vocabulary knowledge by knowing new meanings from chunks of words, being able to understand and use authentic language).

2. Distribute a handout (see the Appendix) that includes example sentences using target collocations. The target collocations could be selected from textbooks or from the References and Further Readings at the end of this activity.

3. Have students read examples individually and guess the meanings of the collocations.

4. Let students exchange their ideas with other classmates (pair/group work).

5. Teach the meanings of the target collocations by explaining the meaning of each word in a collocation first and then the whole meaning of the collocation. Discuss how the collocations are used in the handout and how we can make our own sentences including the collocations.

CAVEATS AND OPTIONS

1. If needed, more examples are available in the Corpus of Contemporary American English (http://corpus.byu.edu/coca). Type the target collocation in the WORD(S) section and click the SEARCH button. You also can use SECTIONS when you teach the use of collocations based on different genres or time periods.

2. As an extension to this activity, ask learners to prepare a worksheet for other members of their class based on a short piece of text that they have selected themselves.

3. Make sure that learners follow up on these activities with opportunities to use the collocations in their speaking and writing.

REFERENCES AND FURTHER READINGS

Collocation lists

EnglishClub: www.englishclub.com/vocabulary/collocations-lists.htm

EnglishLeap: www.englishleap.com/vocabulary/collocations

Collocation dictionary

ProWritingAid: http://prowritingaid.com/Free-Online-Collocations-Dictionary.aspx

Example texts

Corpus of Contemporary American English: http://corpus.byu.edu/coca

Laufer, B., & Girsai, N. (2008). Form-focused instruction in second language vocabulary learning: A case of contrastive analysis and translation. *Applied Linguistics, 29*, 649–716. doi:10.1093/applin/amn018

Webb, S., & Kagimoto, E. (2009). The effects of vocabulary learning on collocation and meaning. *TESOL Quarterly, 43*, 55–77. doi:10.1002/j.1545-7249.2009.tb00227.x

Zimmerman, C. (2008). *Word knowledge: A vocabulary teacher's handbook.* New York, NY: Oxford University Press.

APPENDIX: *Sample Collocations Handout*

What are collocations? "The ways words are combined with each other" (Zimmerman, 2008, p. 37)

Guess the meanings of underlined collocations.

> I went into his office, sat down in the chair. The dentist put a paper napkin around my neck. I opened my mouth and said my back tooth was hurting a lot. He looked at it with a little mirror and asked how I had allowed my teeth to get into that condition.
>
> "I'm going to have to pull it," he said. "You've already lost a few teeth and if you don't <u>undergo</u> <u>treatment</u> fast you're going to lose all the others, including these here," and he gave a strident tap on my front teeth.
>
> Anesthetic injected into the gum. He showed me the tooth at the tip of his forceps. "The root is rotten, see?" he said, indifferently. "That'll be four hundred." What a laugh. "I don't have it, man," I said. "You don't have what?"

> Denver hospital staff informed him there was no hospital backup program in Colorado accepting patients any longer. He was told he would need to go to an Oklahoma facility in three days. Before that surgery, Jason had been living in his own apartment. But he was no longer able to live on his own and was being told he also was no longer able to live in Colorado.
>
> "I was really scared," Jason said last week, lying in a bed at Swedish Medical Center in Englewood, where he is about to <u>undergo</u> another <u>surgery</u> on his back muscles. "All of a sudden, my support system was being taken away."

Delexicalized Verb Collocations

Joshua Brook Antle

Levels	*Beginner*
Aims	*Improve productive ability in using delexicalized verb collocations*
Class Time	*10 minutes*
Preparation Time	*15 minutes*

Delexicalized verbs, such as *have, take,* and *get* are commonly used in English, but their meaning is largely dependent on the words with which they are used. Delexicalized verbs and collocations (Chan & Liou, 2005) are common sources of error for language learners. Students often have receptive knowledge of collocations but lack the productive ability necessary to use them in conversations (Eyckmans, 2009).

PROCEDURE

1. Assign one collocation list for homework each week for 10 weeks. The lists are on the first website mentioned in the References and Further Reading section and are suitable for beginner students.

2. Encourage students to use the collocation dictionary (see References and Further Reading) while completing the assignment.

3. Before the next class, prepare 12 short cloze conversations using the collocations from the homework assignment (an example for List 3 is in the Appendix). Write the answer on the back of each conversation.

4. Place the 12 conversations around the classroom. In pairs, have students read a conversation aloud and fill in the missing collocation. Students can then check their answer and move on to another conversation.

CAVEATS AND OPTIONS

1. To simplify the activity, you can write the 12 collocations for the cloze activity on the board and/or attach the corresponding picture from the collocation dictionary to each conversation.

2. For a follow-up activity, give a pair of students one of the targeted collocations and have them create their own four-line conversation.

REFERENCES AND FURTHER READING

Collocation lists and homework assignments: https://sites.google.com/a/joshua antle.com/english-collocations

Collocation dictionary: https://sites.google.com/a/joshuaantle.com/collocation dictionary/home

Chan, T., & Liou, H.-C. (2005). Effects of web-based concordancing instruction on EFL students' learning of verb–noun collocations. *Computer Assisted Language Learning, 18*, 231–251. doi:10.1080/09588220500185769

Eyckmans, J. (2009). Toward an assessment of learners' receptive and productive syntagmatic knowledge. In A. Barfield & H. Gyllstad (Eds.), *Researching collocations in another language* (pp. 139–152). New York, NY: Palgrave Macmillan.

APPENDIX: *Collocation List Examples*

List 1

Check email	Go out for dinner	Get divorced
Do housework	Get lost	Get married
Have a drink	Make the bed	Have children
Apply for a job	Pay the rent	Get dressed

List 2

Do laundry	Get comfortable	Live together
Be in a good mood	Go online	Pay someone a visit
Come on time	Have a headache	Restart a computer
Get a loan	Have a holiday	Take a bus

List 3

Do some exercise	Get angry	Look for a job
Call an ambulance	Get drunk	Pay well
Come prepared	Go out of business	Save a document
Do nothing	Have an argument	Take a/an (English) class

List 4

Do the cooking	Get a train	Make a difference
Carry out experiments	Get home	Save energy
Come right back	Go out with friends	Take a look
Do someone a favor	Have a problem	Take notes

List 5

Do your homework	Get wet	Make a mistake
Catch a cold	Go overseas	Save electricity
Come to a decision	Have a rest	Take a message
Do the washing up	Keep in touch	Take someone's temperature

List 6

Fall asleep	Get worried	Make an appointment
Catch a plane	Hand in your work	Save money
Delete a file	Have fun	Take an exam
Do your best	Keep quiet	Take your time

List 7

Get ready	Give someone a lift	Make a noise
Catch fire	Have a baby	Save time
Do a search	Have lunch	Take a photo
Do your hair	Live on your own	Visit a website

List 8

Go to bed	Go abroad	Make a reservation
Cause damage	Have a bath	Save something on a computer
Fall in love	Have time	Take a seat
Forward an email	Make someone laugh	Waste time

List 9

Have a nap	Go bad	Open an attachment
Come early	Have a conversation	Spend some time
Feel sick	Install software	Take a taxi
Get a haircut	Make money	Write a prescription

List 10

Make dinner	Go fishing	Pay attention
Come late	Have a good time	Take a break
Find a partner	Keep calm	Take medicine
Get a job	Make someone angry	Write an essay

Examples for List 3

A: What did the doctor say?
B: I need to change my diet and . . .
A: Are you going to join a health club?
B: Yeah. I might try the one in front of Sapporo station.

A: There was a traffic accident in front of the building.
B: Was anyone hurt?
A: Nothing serious, but I . . . just in case.
B: I can hear it coming now.

A: I am going on a day hike with Hiro tomorrow.
B: That should be fun.
A: Yeah, but he never . . . He always drinks from my water bottle and asks for some snacks.

A: I have been so busy this week I just want to . . . this weekend.
B: I can't blame you. You've been working from 9 to 9 every day.
A: Yeah, but next week will be much better.

A: I went to the movies yesterday, and this couple in front of me talked through the whole movie.
B: I hate that. I . . . when that happens.
A: Me too. But I never say anything.

A: What will you do tonight?
B: My friend is visiting from Tokyo. We will go out for a drink.
A: Where to?
B: I'm not sure. I want a quiet night, though. I can't . . . because I have a test tomorrow.

A: Wasn't there an Italian restaurant here before?
B: Yes. It . . . shortly after it opened, though.
A: Do you know why?
B: I don't know. It's a great location.

A: I . . . with my girlfriend.
B: What about?
A: She wants me to help around the house more.

A: How's this semester been going for you?
B: Pretty good. My classes are not too difficult so I have time to . . .
A: Any luck?
B: Yeah. I have an interview next week.

A: How was your interview?
B: Great. They offered me the job.
A: Congratulations! Will you take it?
B: Maybe. It doesn't . . . , but I think I would enjoy it.

A: Can I copy it from your computer?
B: Sure, go ahead.
A: Where did you . . . ?
B: On the desktop.

A: I want to . . . cooking . . .
B: Really. Why?
A: I am moving into my own apartment next month, and my mom usually does the cooking.
B: There's a cooking school in Arisa called ABC Cooking.

Working With Multiword Verbs

Anna Siyanova-Chanturia

Levels	*Intermediate +*
Aims	*Gain awareness of and practice using multiword verbs*
Class Time	*10–15 minutes per activity*
Preparation Time	*10–20 minutes*

Multiword verbs are combinations of a verb and a particle (e.g., *work out, hang out, put off*). Multiword verbs are important because they are extremely common in English. Students will sound more fluent if they learn and use a variety of such verbs. English language learners often avoid using multiword verbs and prefer their one-word equivalents because it is not always clear whether the verb and the particle are separable or not (e.g., *send the letter off/send off the letter*). Also, a multiword verb may have more than one meaning (e.g., *turn in an assignment/she turned him in*), or the same verb may be combined with different particles to form different multiword verbs (e.g., *turn out/turn in/turn off*). All of these reasons may add to students' confusion. In addition, students may find it easier to learn one word (e.g., *postpone*) than two words (e.g., *put off*).

PROCEDURE

1. Select a text you recently used in class, and identify the most common multiword units in the text that you would like to focus on in class. Write the items you have selected on a piece of paper. Make sure to write them with some space around them because you are about to cut up the piece of paper. When they are cut up, you need to make sure you have enough for everyone in your class to have one each.

2. Cut up multiword verbs of your choice into two so that the verb and the particle are on different pieces of paper. The number of pieces of paper should be equal to the number of students in your class.

3. Put the pieces of paper in a bag, mix them, and ask each student to take out one piece of paper. Each student should end up with either a verb or a particle.

4. Ask students to mingle and find their match. For example, if a student has *tell* on his or her piece of paper, that student should find the student who has *off* written on his or hers.

5. Once pairs are formed, each pair should create a sentence with their multi-word verb. Have students either put their sentences on the board for everyone to read or create a poster or a story with all the sentences in them as a class.

CAVEATS AND OPTIONS

1. Make sure that that students have plenty of opportunity to work with the multiword units as whole chunks.

2. Explore multiword verbs in which the verb and the particle are separable as well as inseparable by selecting 10 examples from a text you have used in class. It is also a good idea to use a variety of objects in the sentences (e.g., pronouns as well as nouns), because some multiword verbs behave differently with different objects (e.g., *write it down/*write down it, write my address down/write down my address*). Print out and cut up sentences containing one multiword verb (one word per piece of paper). Put students in teams of two to three, and give each team two to three cut-up sentences. Ask the teams to put the words in the correct order.

3. Ask students to think of as many multiword verbs as they can where the verb is the same but the particle is different (e.g., *get back/up/down/off/in/out, stand back/up/for/out*). Have students create a sentence with each of the multiword verbs which best illustrates its meaning. See if students can spot any common patterns in the use of the same particle with different verbs (e.g., *up* in *stand up* and *get up, back* in *get back* and *stand back*). This activity can be done in pairs, in small groups, or individually.

Showing Your True Colors

Eimile Máiréad Green

Levels	**Upper intermediate to advanced**
Aims	**Use color vocabulary to express emotions**
	Develop fluency
	Develop cross-cultural communication skills
	Enhance collaborative skills
Class Time	**25 minutes**
Preparation Time	**5 minutes**
Resources	**Interview handout (see Appendix)**

PROCEDURE

1. Introduce students to expressions in English which use color to convey emotions. Some examples might be *feeling blue* or being as *white as a sheet*.

2. Have learners discuss the meanings of these expressions and build up a bank of them using a poster on a wall or a page in their vocabulary notebooks.

3. As a review activity, prepare an interview sheet for students on which you provide questions using these fixed expressions of color (see the Appendix for an example).

4. Model the interview task with a student. Have the student ask a question from the interview handout, to which you respond using the highlighted color vocabulary.

5. Explain to students that they will take turns conducting an interview to learn more about each other. Give everyone a copy of the interview questions, and provide some time for students to prepare their answers to the questions in the interview sheet individually. About 10 minutes should be enough.

6. Place students in pairs.

7. Distribute the interview handout (see the Appendix).

8. Have students work in pairs to conduct interviews using the prompts provided on the handout.

CAVEATS AND OPTIONS

1. This activity works best as a review of previously studied color vocabulary.

2. You can choose to substitute other color expressions (e.g., *blue in the face, a gray area*) depending on the vocabulary items that were covered in earlier lessons.

3. For less advanced students, the number of color expressions can be reduced.

4. For more advanced students, students can conduct research on a chosen color expression and share findings with the class.

5. For larger classes, students can conduct interviews in small-group settings rather than in pairs.

6. Time permitting, students can share the most interesting interview responses with the whole class.

7. As an extension, students can choose the most interesting interview response and write a story based on the response.

REFERENCES AND FURTHER READING

BBC. (2013). The Teacher: Series 4—Colour Idioms. *BBC Learning English.* Retrieved from http://www.bbc.co.uk/worldservice/learningenglish/language/theteacher

APPENDIX: *The Interview*

With a partner, take turns conducting an interview to learn more about each other.

Tell me about . . .

- a time when you were **green with envy**.
- a time when you **got the blues**.
- a time when you were **tickled pink**.
- **a red-letter day.**
- **a shrinking violet** in your family.
- a time when you turned **white as a sheet**.
- a time when you were **green around the gills**.
- a time when you were **in the dark**.
- something that makes you **see red**.
- something that happened **out of the blue**.
- a color idiom in your first language.

Songs and Gap-Fill Reloaded

Friederike Tegge

Levels	*Low-intermediate +*
Aims	*Consolidate formulas and collocations in an authentic context*
	Practice listening
Class Time	*20 minutes*
Preparation Time	*20 minutes*
Resources	*Song (CD, MP3)*
	Audio player

PROCEDURE

1. Find a song that you think your class will enjoy and make sure you have an accurate copy of the lyrics. Look for high-frequency formulas and idioms in the song you have chosen, because they try to convey in few words a generalizable meaning that a broad audience can relate to. For example, Dolly Parton's "9 to 5" contains formulas such as *drive you crazy* and *they are out to get me*. Nickelback's "If Today Was Your Last Day" contains useful expressions like *don't take the free ride*.

2. Hand out a gap-fill version of a song with one word of each target formula or collocation missing (e.g., *It's enough to _____ you crazy*). Have students listen to the song and fill in the gaps.

3. After listening at least twice, have students discuss their answers and, as a class, check the answers together.

4. Play the song again so the students, now aware of the correct answers, can test and practice their listening comprehension.

5. Do a different activity related or unrelated to the song. For example, discuss the topic of the song, talk about personal experiences, and so on. Inserting another activity allows for distributed retrieval, which is more effective than massed practice.

6. Collect the song lyrics from students.

7. Hand out another gap-fill version of the lyrics, with the entire formula missing (*It's enough to* _____ _____ _____). Have students fill in the gaps from memory. This activity gets students to retrieve the multiword units from memory (for more about retrieval, see Baddeley, Eysenck, & Anderson, 2009).

8. Discuss the correct answers. If no explicit feedback is provided, false memory may persist. Students will be keen to know what slipped their mind.

9. Listen to the song again. Even better, sing along!

CAVEATS AND OPTIONS

1. Depending on learners' proficiency, you can delete more or less text.

2. Do or repeat the second extended gap-fill in a subsequent lesson.

REFERENCES AND FURTHER READING

Baddeley, A., Eysenck, M. W., & Anderson, M. C. (2009). *Memory*. Hove, England: Psychology Press.

Kroeger, C. (2008). If today was your last day. *Dark Horse*. Vancouver, British Columbia, Canada: Roadrunner.

Parton, D. (1980). 9 to 5. *9 to 5 and odd jobs*. Nashville, TN: RCA.

Consolidating Vocabulary Learning

- **Consolidating Meaning**
- **Consolidating Form**
- **Working on Meaning and Form**
- **Organizing Vocabulary Learning**

Part II: Consolidating Vocabulary Learning

The focus in this part is on consolidating vocabulary knowledge after the first encounter with words. Specifically, the focus is on those important subsequent meetings with lexical items which help build learners' conceptualizations of meaning, form, and use. Recognizing words in context is one thing; being able to produce words accurately and fluently in the right context in speaking or writing is quite another. Learning a new word can be a complex task in a second language because there are many possible aspects of knowledge to think about. The most obvious is the meaning of a word. Nation (2014) suggests that the form and the use of a word are two other main concepts to consider when it comes to learning a word. Table 1 outlines the aspects of knowledge relating to form, meaning, and use to consider when producing a word in writing.

You can think about how those focus questions in Table 1 might change when the focus is on the knowledge that students need in order to recognize words.

TABLE 1. KNOWLEDGE REQUIRED FOR PRODUCTION OF A WORD IN SPEAKING AND WRITING

Knowledge of What?	Aspect	Focus Questions
Form	Speaking	How is the word pronounced?
	Written	How is the word written and spelled?
	Word parts	What word parts are needed to express the meaning?
Meaning	Form and meaning	What word form can be used to express this meaning?
	Concepts and referents	What items can this concept refer to?
	Associations	What other words could we use instead of this one?
Use	Grammatical function	In what patterns must we use this word?
	Collocations	What words or types of words must we use with this one?
	Constraints of use (register, frequency, etc.)	Where, when, and how often can we use this word?

Source: Adapted from Nation (2014, p. 49).

So, for reading, a question for collocations might be "What words or types of words might we see occurring together?" Keep in mind that vocabulary learning is incremental in nature (Schmitt, 2010), which means learners do not tend to learn everything about a vocabulary item in the first meeting. Instead, they build up their knowledge and expertise about different aspects of knowledge of a word. In other words, they consolidate their knowledge of items that they already know something about.

Making time for revision of vocabulary in class can help with consolidating vocabulary knowledge. Dealing with vocabulary revision in a systematic way helps learners and teachers find gaps in learners' knowledge of a word, which can help with setting goals for filling those gaps. It can help learners and teachers figure out any problems, such as confusing two vocabulary items in terms of meaning or form. It can also help determine how learners are progressing with their vocabulary learning overall.

A common theme in this section is that students require a large amount of repetition (see Webb, 2007) with lexical items to help build memory of words and multiword units as well as build vocabulary size. Another common theme is some form of competition in review activities to lift learners' motivation and encourage speedier retrieval of form or meaning. Note also that many activities in this section have learners working in groups to achieve vocabulary goals. A final point in this section is the importance of practice for vocabulary knowledge. Just like learning a complex task such as driving a car, theory can take you only so far. At some point, you have to get in the car and actually practice your driving skills. Providing opportunities to use lexical items in writing and speaking is an important classroom task, because this practice helps learners with language use and control. It also provides opportunities for feedback on use, which in turn can help with developing accuracy. This part ends with some ideas on how a teacher might organize and assess vocabulary learning in their courses.

REFERENCES

Nation, I. S. P. (2014). *Learning vocabulary in another language* (2nd ed.). Cambridge, England: Cambridge University Press.

Schmitt, N. (2010). *Researching vocabulary*. Basingstoke, England: Palgrave Macmillan.

Webb, S. (2007). The effects of repetition on vocabulary knowledge. *Applied Linguistics, 28*, 46–65. doi:10.1093/applin/aml048

What Am I Thinking Of?

Christopher Gordon

Levels	*Any*
Aims	*Consolidate previously learned vocabulary*
	Learn new words in the same category
Class Time	*5–10 minutes*
Preparation Time	*2 minutes*

The first time this game is played, it might be useful to have pictures of the vocabulary items. This game is fun for English language learners of all ages and proficiencies, with the difficulty being controlled by both teacher and students.

PROCEDURE

1. Choose a category of words that you want students to practice (e.g., animals, food).

2. Tell the class that you are thinking of a word from the chosen category.

3. Give students a hint about the word that you are thinking of.

4. Have students raise their hands to guess the word.

5. Continue to give students hints until one of the students gets the correct answer.

   This is an example of a typical round of this game:

   T: I am thinking of an animal. This animal is big.

   S1: An elephant.

   T: No, it's not an elephant.

   S2: A lion.

   T: No, sorry.

   S3: A bear.

   T: No. This animal doesn't have any legs.

S4: A snake.

T: No.

S5: A fish.

T: No, but this animal does live in water.

S6: A whale.

T: Yes, I am thinking of a whale.

CAVEATS AND OPTIONS

1. After students are familiar with the game, the student who gets the correct answer can come to the front of the class and think of his or her own word from the category that is being taught. The other students in the class try to guess what the student is thinking of. For younger students it is a good idea for you to ask the student what he or she is thinking of before starting the game to make sure that the student does not change the word if someone guesses it. If it is required, you could help the student give hints to the class.

2. If you know some of the students' native language, students could give some answers in their native language and you could tell them what they are in English. This method can be really beneficial because students can learn words that they are interested in learning.

3. This game can also be done as a team activity, where the class is divided into teams and they have to guess what word the other team is thinking about. The activity can also be done in groups or pairs where the students take turns thinking of a word.

4. If the class is having difficulty in guessing what word the person is thinking of, you should give big hints so that students can guess what it is.

Slap the Board

Heather Roberts

Levels	*Any*
Aims	*Review vocabulary*
Class Time	*10 minutes*
Preparation Time	*2 minutes*
Resources	*Board, pens/chalk, duster, list of vocabulary words*

PROCEDURE

1. Wake up a sluggish class! Push furniture aside so there is a good space between desks/tables and the board.

2. Form two teams.

3. Teams stand equidistant from the board and a reasonable space from each other.

4. Write about 15 of the words being studied at random on the board. Words should be spaced some distance from each other.

5. Close all vocabulary books and dictionaries.

6. Teams choose their first "runners."

7. Give the meaning, a synonym, antonym, description, and so on of one of words on the board.

8. The runners must run to the board and slap the word they think is the answer.

9. Repeat the process with different runners until all the words have been slapped.

10. The winning team is the one with the most correct answers/slaps.

CAVEATS AND OPTIONS

1. This can be a noisy game.

2. Warn students that there should be no touching (shoving, pushing, etc.) of other team members.

3. Make sure every team member gets a turn at being the runner.

Memories

Helen Howarth

Levels	***Pre-intermediate+***
Aims	***Consolidate the learning of definitions or collocations***
Class Time	***10–15 minutes***
Preparation Time	***15 minutes***

This activity aids learning by encouraging learners to remember, search for, and say collocations or definitions. Less preparation is required if words are already entered into Quizlet (see Part V: Vocabulary and Technology).

PROCEDURE

1. Have about 15 matching pairs of word cards; they could be word/definition or word/collocation (with a gap where the collocation should be; see below).

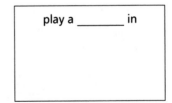

2. Divide the class into groups of two to six students.

3. Place the cards face up on the table, then match them. This activity will elicit some useful discussion about the words and make sure that everyone actually knows the correct match. Quickly check that this is correct before proceeding to the next step.

4. When students are confident they know the matching pairs, sort the cards into two groups: the word and the definition or collocation. Have students turn the piles upside down and mix them up. Students then take turns picking up one card from each pile. If it is a matching pair, they keep the pair and have another turn. If it is not a matching pair, the cards are put back into the same place, and it is then the next player's turn.

CAVEATS AND OPTIONS

1. An intermediate step between Steps 3 and 4 is to remove the cards with the words on them, and students take turns picking up a card with the meaning or gapped collocation and produce the target word. The other students decide whether this is the correct answer.

2. Encourage students to say the words and meanings or collocations as they play, because this reinforces learning aurally and provides an opportunity to practise the pronunciation.

3. Cards can also be used to match pairs of students for another activity. Randomly hand out cards to students, which they use to search for their partner.

4. It is important to check answers carefully because matching activities can be prone to confusing learners if they make the incorrect match. Incorrect associations are likely to linger in the memory, unfortunately.

Productive Vocabulary Party

Kristen Sharma

Levels	*Beginning to advanced*
Aims	*Use vocabulary productively to aid learning of meaning and collocations*
Class Time	*15 minutes*
Preparation Time	*30 minutes*
Resources	*A question, including a target word, for each student to memorise*

This activity is a good way to introduce weekly vocabulary, showing students how to use the target words productively.

PROCEDURE

1. Before class, identify the target words.

2. Create a question which uses each of the target words. For example, if the target word is *achieve*, the question could be "What do you hope to achieve on this course?" (See the examples in the Appendix.)

3. Collate all the questions on a document in at least 14-point font, making the target words bold. Print this document, and cut it up so each strip of paper has a question on it.

4. In class, once you have introduced the words, give each student a strip of paper with a question on it.

5. Explain that the class will have a vocabulary party. They must memorise their question, then mix and mingle with their classmates, asking each other their questions in a natural way, without reading.

6. They should answer their classmates' questions as fully as they can, using the target vocabulary.

7. Once students have asked their question to three people, they can swap questions with another student. They then memorise the new question and mix and mingle again to ask their classmates that question.

8. You decide when it is time to end the activity.

CAVEATS AND OPTIONS

The strips of paper with the questions on them can be collected and stuck to the wall for future reference, especially in terms of grammar or collocations with particular words. As you do this activity more and more, a bank of questions can be built up, reducing the preparation time.

REFERENCES AND FURTHER READING

Coxhead, A. (1998). *An academic word list* (Occasional Publication No. 18). Victoria, New Zealand: University of Wellington.

APPENDIX: *Academic Word List Question Bank*

I have created a bank of questions based on the Academic Word List (Coxhead, 1998) for use in my course, set out in the following format:

Word	Sublist	Question
Access	4	How do I **access** my student email account?
Accommodate	9	Can you describe your current **accommodation**?
		Do you think your university **accommodates** international students' cultural needs enough?
Accompany	8	Did anyone **accompany** you when you first came to New Zealand?
Accumulate	8	How can we stop the **accumulation** of carbon dioxide in the atmosphere?
Accurate	6	How can you make your grammar more **accurate**?

Rating and Raising Word Knowledge

Mark Wolfersberger

Levels	Intermediate to advanced
Aims	Increase knowledge of specific words through interaction with other students
Class Time	10 minutes
Preparation Time	5 minutes

The purpose of this activity is for students to teach each other what they know about a set of vocabulary words. By teaching each other, everyone learns more. Students who do not know a word learn basic information about it. Students who know the word become more familiar with it by recalling what they know and then explaining it to another student. This is a great activity to use in place of the teacher defining and explaining every word to the whole class.

PROCEDURE

1. Write on the board a list of 6–10 vocabulary words that everyone in class is going to study.

2. Students write down each word and use the following scale to rate their knowledge level of each word (see Allen, 1999). Be sure that students write a rating beside each word.

   1 = I have never seen or heard this word.

   2 = I have seen or heard the word but don't know what it means.

   3 = I think I know a meaning for the word.

   4 = I can explain the meaning of the word and use it in a sentence.

3. After students rate each word, they move around the room and discuss the words with other students. If a student rated a word 1, 2, or 3, he or she should find a student who rated the word a 4. Students who have a 4 rating next to a word should be prepared to explain the word to other students. The goal of students' discussions is to learn more about the aspects of the words they do not yet know.

4. While students are talking to each other and learning words, direct students with a lower rating on a word to other students who have a 4 rating for the same word.

5. If you find that no students know a particular word, you can explain the word to several students. Then those students explain the word to the remainder of students in the class.

CAVEATS AND OPTIONS

1. Move around the room and look at students' ratings at the beginning of the activity when students are rating the words on the list. This monitoring will help you identify words that most students do not know and that you may need to help with.

2. The first few times you try this activity, you will likely find that most students will overestimate their knowledge of a word. Students may rate most or all of the words on the list as a 4, but then find that they cannot explain the words to other students. In this case, remind students that a 4 rating means that they can explain the word to other people and that their rating should really be a 3.

3. As students are talking to each other about word meanings, it is important that you listen to their conversations. Some students are skeptical that their peers really know a word, and you may need to confirm that a student is giving the correct meaning. Additionally, words have multiple meanings and students may know a meaning that is different from the meaning you intend for them to learn. Occasionally, you may need to correct a student who thinks he or she knows a word but does not.

4. If you are using a list of words that students are mostly familiar with or would like to increase the depth of word knowledge in the activity, you can add a level 5 to the ratings. Level 5 can be related to different aspects of word knowledge beyond a simple definition. For example, it could be related to multiple meanings, collocations, connotation, or word family. Here are some examples:

   5 = I know three collocations for this word and can demonstrate them in example sentences.

   5 = I know more than one meaning for this word and can explain them to someone.

5 = I understand the meaning of this word and can explain it to someone.

5 = I know two different forms of this word (noun, verb, adjective, adverb) and can correctly pronounce them.

REFERENCES AND FURTHER READING

Allen, J. (1999). *Words, words, words: Teaching vocabulary in grades 4–12*. York, ME: Stenhouse.

Back to the Board

Natalia Petersen

Levels	*Any*
Aims	*Explain word meaning under pressure*
Class Time	*15 minutes+*
Preparation Time	*None*
Resources	*List of 10–15 words*

This game requires previous study of the target words. Depending on the level of the class, the words could come from the weekly vocabulary list. It is good as a last-minute review before a test, because it requires students to think on their feet and use the English in their heads. Twelve to sixteen students is a good number of participants, but smaller or larger groups could work, too.

PROCEDURE

1. Divide the class into four teams, or three with fewer students.

2. Place four chairs in front of the board facing away from it and as far away from each other as possible.

3. Draw four boxes on the board.

4. Ask students to think of a name for their team and write these over the boxes.

5. Ask one student from each team to sit on the chair facing away from the board. The rest of the team stands in front of him or her.

6. Write a target word on the board.

7. The standing team members have to explain the meaning of the word to the person who can't see it. The team members can use mime, part of speech, word stress (hummed or clapped), collocations or sentences (with a beep for the missing word) to help the sitting person guess the word. But they cannot use family words, because that makes it too easy.

8. When the sitting person knows the meaning, he or she calls it out. If the student is right, he or she gets a point in the team's box.

9. Have students change teams and continue.

10. Stop when everyone in each team has had several opportunities to be in the "hot seat" or when it gets too noisy.

11. The team with the most points wins.

CAVEATS AND OPTIONS

1. It can be difficult to hear the answers. Have a student helper adjudicate.

2. Add in pronunciation. If the word isn't pronounced correctly, the team doesn't get a point.

3. Allocate enough points for the last round so that all teams have a chance of winning.

4. Use the game to review words covered in previous weeks, not just the weekly class list before the weekly test.

5. Have a system in place to deal with any accusations of cheating.

REFERENCES AND FURTHER READING

Scrivener, J. (1994). *Learning teaching.* Oxford, England: Macmillan.

Picture Tic-Tac-Toe

Solihin Agyl

Levels	*Higher elementary to intermediate*
Aims	*Practice vocabulary daily using a fun, real-life communication activity*
Class Time	*30 minutes*
Preparation Time	*20–30 minutes*
Resources	*Dice*
	Tic-Tac-Toe grid (a 3 x 3 grid)
	18 pictures on cards
	Small pieces of paper to use as X and O

Prior to class, you can prepare the resources and have a simulation with fellow teachers to make sure the activity works well. Use 9 pictures for the first round and the other 9 for the next round in case students need more. In class, you can provide any kind of pictures. Copy all 18 pictures for all pairs. You can also prepare the vocabulary through pictures on cards to be distributed in class. Pictures should generally cover vocabulary the students have been learning.

PROCEDURE

1. Distribute all the cards to the class. Let students think of the vocabulary which may come up from the pictures.

2. Pair up the students. Let them face the Tic-Tac-Toe grid, shuffle the cards, and put each of the 9 cards face down on the grid while the other 9 are piled face down outside the grid. Have students choose which one will use an X and which one will use an O for their Tic-Tac-Toe cards.

3. To start the activity, each pair should roll the dice. The person with the highest score of the dice can pick up one card and show the picture. She or he has to tell a short story of her or his own experience based on the picture. While the story is being told, the partner can ask questions.

4. The activity continues with the next person. This activity enables each pair to ask each other questions to elaborate on what they want to know about each partner's experience; a natural dialogue happens. Students will enjoy a sense of competition, and the first person who can put three X (crosses) or O (noughts) in line either horizontally, vertically, or diagonally is the winner.

CAVEATS AND OPTIONS

1. This activity can also be applied for lower levels but with shorter stories with simple sentences and with no questions after the story has been told.

2. The total number of students for this activity is 20.

REFERENCES AND FURTHER READING

Oxford, R. L. (1990). *Language learning strategies: What every teacher should know*. Boston, MA: Heinle & Heinle.

Using Crosswords to Review Vocabulary

Sonia Millett

Levels	*Any*
Aims	*Recycle and review vocabulary*
Class Time	*20 minutes+*
Preparation Time	*30 minutes*
Resources	*Crosswords using free online software*

Crosswords are a great way to recycle and reinforce vocabulary. Students love the challenge of completing the puzzle first. There is a heads-down, focused atmosphere if done individually, and if done in pairs with an English-only rule or with different first language partners, there is a buzz of negotiation about spelling, meaning, and grammar. Make your own crosswords using free online software. The beauty of online sites is that you choose the set of words. Some sites supply a definition, whereas others let you tailor the clues to your own requirements. Answers are generated by the software. One useful site is EclipseCrossword (www.eclipsecrossword.com). Download the programme and follow the simple instructions.

PROCEDURE

1. Create a crossword

2. Hand out copies.

3. Sit back and relax.

4. Or tactfully help students who might be struggling. Don't fall into the trap of being too helpful. This is the perfect time for you to hand the task over to students and not interfere. They can ask other students for help.

CAVEATS AND OPTIONS

1. Pairs work well. Avoid having three students working on one crossword. There's always one who can't see the paper properly and will lose interest.

2. It's important that students sit side by side so they can both see the puzzle and clues clearly.

3. Adjust the level of difficulty by including a word bank or not.

4. Students who finish first can give each other a spelling quiz on the words or help other students. Help means giving extra clues, not telling them the answers.

5. The activity can be done in groups. Make one large copy of the crossword grid per table and give everyone a copy of the clues.

6. Include a listening component by having students sit opposite each other and read out the clues to their partner, who writes in the answers. Change roles with across and down clues.

7. Crosswords can be turned into a team game with the grid displayed on a whiteboard. You read out the clues, teams answer by turns, and you write in the answers in different team colours. The team with the most squares wins.

8. Crosswords may be used at any level. They are successful with high-level academic students as well as with students with low levels of literacy, such as learners with refugee backgrounds. For these students you can make a puzzle using the names of family members, simple around-the-house words, and shopping words.

Vocabulary Champ

Sonia Millett

Levels	**Beginning to intermediate**
Aims	**Recycle vocabulary in use**
Class Time	**20 minutes+**
Preparation Time	**10 minutes**
Resources	**A reusable grid (see Appendix)**
	Six words currently being studied in class

This game is a good way to put target words into productive written use. It also focuses on words in context and grammatical accuracy.

PROCEDURE

1. Write all the students' names in the first column of the grid (see Appendix).

2. Write the target words along the top row.

3. Sit at the front of the room with the grid.

4. Students close all their vocabulary books and dictionaries.

5. Explain that everyone has to write his or her own perfect sentence using the words you give them.

6. Write the first word on the board so that all students can see it.

7. Students write a sentence using the word, then bring it up for you to check.

8. If the sentence is meaningful and grammatically correct, they get a tick on the grid and can start on the next word.

9. The first student to get a tick writes the next word on the board.

10. If the sentence is not perfect, do not mark it but send the student back to think about it and make it right.

11. Students cannot start on the next word until their first sentence is perfect.

12. The first student to get six ticks becomes the Vocab Champ.

CAVEATS AND OPTIONS

1. It is important that you do not correct wrong sentences. The idea is that students think about their sentences and correct them themselves.

2. This activity works well with a class of around 12 students. If there are many more, you can't check all the sentences quickly enough.

3. The Vocab Champ(s) can help other students with their sentences.

4. Adjust the difficulty level of this activity by including a grammar structure (e.g., word + past tense, word + passive, word + *if*).

APPENDIX: *Vocab Champ Grid*

Name	Word						VocabChamp
	1 achieve	2 reason	3 adult	4 healthy	5 succeed	6 guess	
Takihisa							
Mavis							
Bo Shi							
Ahmed							
Junko							
Henry							
Fadumo							
Yitong							
Lennon							
Thanh							

Quizzes for Vocabulary Cards

Tomoko Antle

Levels	*Any*
Aims	*Improve receptive and productive abilities for high-interest words*
Class Time	*10 minutes*
Preparation Time	*5 minutes*
Resources	*Vocabulary cards (see Appendix)*
	Dictionaries (see References and Further Reading)

This is a pair-work activity using word cards. Word cards are an efficient way to learn vocabulary because they allow learners to focus on individual words and repeatedly expose themselves to the targeted words (Nation, 2001).

PROCEDURE

1. Have students create several word cards (see Caveats and Options for information about the number of cards). With your assistance, students can decide which words they want to target. The words can be from textbooks used in class, other reading materials, vocabulary that comes up during speaking activities, or entirely student chosen.

2. Have students write the word on top of an index card. Instruct students to use their dictionaries and the resources listed in Step 1 to include pronunciations, definitions, example sentences, collocations, translations, pictures, or word forms on their word cards.

3. After they have completed several cards, have students exchange their word cards with a partner.

4. Student A will choose one card and quiz student B. Student A can ask for a translation, an example sentence using the word, or any other piece of information on the card.

5. If student B answers all of the questions to student A's satisfaction, the card goes into Pile 2.

6. If student B cannot answer all of the questions, the card goes back into the original pile.

7. If a student correctly answers all of the questions about a card from Pile 2, the card can be moved to a third pile.

8. Repeat the process of creating new word cards once or twice a week. The total number of cards will increase over time; however, students do not have to quiz each other on every card. Have students focus on the cards in Pile 1, and use Piles 2 and 3 to review the previously learnt vocabulary.

CAVEATS AND OPTIONS

1. This activity works best if it is frequently done for short periods of time. For example, the cards in Pile 1 should be used for quizzes several times per week. The cards in Pile 2 should be used once every 1 or 2 weeks. This third pile should be used once a month to ensure that students retain the word knowledge.

2. The quiz can be done as a warm-up activity or as an activity to finish a lesson. It can also be used for pairs of students who finish an activity before the rest of the class.

3. Have students prepare only three word cards initially. In the next class, check the cards to ensure that students are choosing useful vocabulary, writing descriptive sentences, and including enough information about the targeted word. If students' first three cards are okay, they can create eight to ten new cards each week as homework or as an in-class activity.

REFERENCES AND FURTHER READING

Cambridge Advanced Learner's Dictionary: http://dictionary.cambridge.org /dictionary/british

Merriam-Webster online dictionary: http://www.merriam-webster.com

Ozdic online collocation dictionary: http://www.ozdic.com

Nation, P. (2001). *Learning vocabulary in another language.* Cambridge, England: Cambridge University Press.

APPENDIX: *Example Word Card*

Front

> **Future** /ˈfjuːtʃə(r)/
>
> (noun) a time after the present
>
> Collocations:
>
> > plan for the ~
> >
> > near ~
> >
> > bright ~
> >
> > great ~
>
> He has a great **future** as a banker.

Back

> (Translation)

Smurf the Words

Winda Hapsari

Levels	*Intermediate*
Aims	*Practice guessing the word/phrase in context*
	Review vocabulary
Class Time	*10–12 minutes*
Preparation Time	*None*
Resources	*Slips of paper (20 cm x 5 cm each)*

PROCEDURE

1. Provide a topic or theme for students to help them consider vocabulary they want to review and possible sentences they can write for this activity. The theme or topic can relate to a previous lesson.

2. Put students into pairs, sitting face to face. One is Student A, the other is Student B.

3. Give each student five or six slips of paper.

4. Ask students to write sentences on the slips of paper that contain vocabulary they have learned previously. They write only one sentence per slip of paper.

5. Have students underline the word or phrase that they want their partner to guess later (see the example in the Appendix). Please note that students should not show their sentences to each other.

6. When all students have finished writing their sentences, they are ready to start talking. Student A starts by reading one sentence to Student B. They are to say "SMURF" for the underlined word. One SMURF is for one word. So if a phrase to be guessed consists of two words, they have to say "SMURF SMURF." For example:

We should not keep grudges against people; everybody makes mistakes.➔	We should not keep "SMURF" against people; everybody makes mistakes.
Santi and I have forgiven each other, and now we are starting over our friendship.➔	Santi and I have forgiven each other, and now we are "SMURF SMURF" our friendship.

7. Students take turns guessing the SMURF word. For each word or phrase to be guessed, students get two chances. If after two guesses they cannot guess the word or phrase, the other student is to tell them the answer.

8. For each word or phrase guessed, students get one point. The winner in each pair is the one with more points.

CAVEATS AND OPTIONS

1. In order to avoid wild guessing, students should create sentences that give clues to the SMURF word/phrase.

2. If you have teenage students who like to do movement activities, you can ask them to stand up and walk around to find five or six students who can guess the SMURF words or phrases. In this case, students start with the first person and read out the sentence (remembering to say SMURF for the word/phrase to be guessed). If that person cannot guess the word, they have to find someone else. If that person can guess the word, they give the paper to him or her. If that person cannot guess the word, the first student with the slip of paper moves on to someone else and tries again. The winner is the first student who can give out all slips of paper in his or her hand.

3. This activity is better done as a warm-up activity in the beginning of a learning session. Besides the function to refresh students' memory of previously learned key vocabulary, the movement and interaction will boost students' engagement in learning.

4. There is a possibility that students will not remember the vocabulary they learned previously. This may especially happen in EFL settings where students have English classes once or twice a week and they do not get enough exposure of English in daily life. In this case, you can provide a short passage on a relevant topic that includes some of the key vocabulary. Have students do silent reading for few minutes before doing SMURF the Words. This activity aims to build students' schemata on what they are about to do. Take back the text when students are about to do the SMURF game.

APPENDIX: *Example Slip of Paper for SMURF Game*

Topic of last session: Forgiving people

Vocabulary learned: *grudges, offenders, disappointment, disappointed, hurt, start over,* etc.

| We should not keep grudges against people. Everybody makes mistakes |
| Even though I am disappointed because he broke his promise, I still put on a smile when I meet him. |

Let's Describe the Word!

Yangting (Tina) Wang

Levels	*High intermediate to low advanced*
Aims	*Engage in self-assessment and review of vocabulary*
	Describe words by their part of speech, synonyms, and antonyms, and by making up sentences
	Develop awareness of the metacognition of the words
	Become more familiar with the categorization of the word
Class Time	*20 minutes*
Preparation Time	*30 minutes*
Resources	*Words from students' textbook*

The classroom game is inspired by catchphrase (http://en.wikipedia.org/wiki/Catchphrase).

PROCEDURE

1. Divide the class into two teams.

2. Before class, choose 150 words students have learned in the textbook. Among these words, 50 should belong to one of the following three categories: animal, agriculture, astrology. Each team will choose one category. They will not see the 50 words in the category.

3. Have students stand in lines. The first person in the line from each team comes to the front of the room, facing the class. Fifty words in the category will be presented one by one in a PowerPoint. The laptop will be facing the blackboard. Only the student who describes the words can see the screen of the laptop. Other students who are in line and guessing will not be able to see.

4. The first person in line describes the first word from the 50 words. For instance, for *carnivore*, the student may say, "It is a noun. It refers to animals that eat meat. It is similar to predator." The other members in the team need to guess the word and shout it out. The person who is describing the word

cannot spell or give different forms of the word. He or she can only answer yes or no when the team members shout out a word. If it is correct, the first person can hit the button and go to the next slide. If it is not correct, he or she will have one more chance to describe a word. He or she can hit the button and go to the next slide to try to describe the second word.

5. If the first person fails to get the team to guess the word, he or she goes to the end of the line and the second person comes to the front and describes the next word from the PowerPoint list. Then the second person goes to the end of the line and the third person continues.

6. The team members take turns in describing the word; they need to guess fast in order to finish the 50 words. The team that finishes the most words in 8 minutes wins.

7. For a follow-up activity, give students a handout (see Appendix), and have them work in pairs after class to write down the words they didn't get right. They need to look the words up in the dictionary and figure out the best way to describe each word and the use of the word. They hand in their completed handout in the next class.

CAVEATS AND OPTIONS

1. Some students may react slowly in the game and get a bit frustrated. You can inform students about the vocabulary game activity several days beforehand and encourage them to review words they learned in the textbook.

2. Because two teams describe and guess words at the same time, they may get distracted by one another. You can have one team go first and the other team be the audience, then switch roles. This vocabulary game is interesting not only to play, but also to watch. Being the audience can help two teams to learn from each other and be familiar with the words that the other team is guessing.

3. You can also divide the teams into boys and girls if there is an even number of each. Grouping students based on their gender and interests can make the game more fun and challenging. Students will enjoy the game while learning and guessing the words.

4. Some words found in the textbook may be difficult for students to understand, such as *horticulture* or *cultivation*. Some words may be hard to describe, such as *crops* or *crocodile*. In the follow-up activity, you can recommend that students look up these difficult words in the Oxford dictionary or on Wikipedia and write their answers in the handout in the Appendix. Students

will learn the part of speech, meaning, synonyms, and how to make up a sentence with the word, which can help them be more familiar with understanding and describing the difficult words they encounter in the game.

APPENDIX: *Handout of the Follow-Up Activity*

Vocabulary	Part of Speech	Meaning in English	Synonym/Antonym	Make Up Sentences

Swat It!

Christopher Gordon

Levels	***Beginning children***
Aims	***Consolidate vocabulary learning***
Class Time	***10–15 minutes***
Preparation Time	***2 minutes***
Resources	***Flash cards with the target vocabulary, either pictures or words***
	Two plastic fly swatters
	Whiteboard

This game can be great fun to play with children of all ages, and it is possible to use any set of vocabulary items to do this activity.

PROCEDURE

1. Attach the flash cards showing the target vocabulary to a whiteboard; the more cards, the harder the game is.

2. Divide the class into two teams.

3. Have one student from each team come to the whiteboard, and give each of them a fly swatter.

4. Tell the students that when you say one of the vocabulary items, they have to hit the corresponding card on the whiteboard with their fly swatter.

5. Ask the students to turn their backs to the whiteboard. Count down from three and then call out one of the vocabulary items. The student who turns round and swats the correct flash card the fastest is the winner. The winning student gets one point for his or her team.

CAVEATS AND OPTIONS

1. If you do not have fly swatters, then the game can be played by asking students to turn round and grab the corresponding flash card rather than swatting it.

2. After students are familiar with how the game works, they can take turns being the "teacher" by calling out the vocabulary item that the participants must try to swat.

3. You can adjust the level of difficulty of the game. To make the game easier, you can attach fewer flash cards to the board or use pictures on the cards. To make the game harder, you can use more flash cards or use words on the cards instead of pictures.

4. The time that this game takes to play can be adapted to meet your needs by varying the amount of time that each pair plays. For example, each pair may play once or best of three depending on the time available.

5. You can get members of the class who are not playing the game to participate in the activity by asking them if the person playing the game has hit the correct flash card. The students who are not playing can also be encouraged to help their teammate if he or she is having difficulty locating the correct flash card.

Text Grab

John Rogers

Levels	*Beginner to advanced*
Aims	*Consolidate vocabulary learning*
	Review vocabulary learning from a listening done in a previous class
Class Time	*10 minutes*
Preparation Time	*Varies*
Resources	*Audio recording from course book*
	Set of vocabulary cards for each group of students

PROCEDURE

1. Before class, identify a number of vocabulary items (words or phrases) from a listening track that you would like to review. See the Appendix for an example of a text with target words underlined.

2. Prepare cards or slips of paper with one word or phrase on each. You will need one set of cards for each group in the class. The number of cards in each set will vary according to the length of the listening text and the level of the learners. Around 8 words or phrases is a good starting point with intermediate learners. This number can be reduced or increased with shorter and longer listenings and/or with learners of lower or higher proficiency levels. The cards should not be too small. Remember that learners should be able to read the words or phrases comfortably and be able to quickly grab the card or slip of paper. Around 12 words or phrases per slip of paper is a good rule of thumb, though this can be adjusted at your discretion.

3. For a prelistening task, in pairs or groups of three, have students first arrange the cards in alphabetical order with some space between each of the cards.

4. While listening to the audio, students compete with the other members of their group to be the first to grab the card when they hear the word or phrase written on the card. The student with the most cards at the end of the listening wins. To provide students with the opportunity to check that they got it right, you can either play the recording again or refer students to the tapescript.

CAVEATS AND OPTIONS

1. This activity can be modified according to the level of the students. With beginner-level learners, relatively few cards should be used. With more advanced classes, more cards can be made and used as the listening tracks increase in length.

2. This activity can be extended in a number of ways, including playing the recording again and asking learners to put the vocabulary words into the order that they hear them. Learners can then use the words to recreate the recording in their own words.

3. Another option with mixed-ability classes is to ask students to only touch or point at the cards when they hear them while the recording is played the first time. Then the recording can be played again following the procedure outlined above. This way, learners might be able to better orient themselves to the listening text. Furthermore, staging the activity like so would hopefully prevent the results from being too lopsided in favor of stronger learner(s).

APPENDIX: *Sample Text*

A text grab is an easy way to ensure that the students remain focused and active during any listening activity and have a bit of fun in the process.

The procedure is simple: Find a text of suitable length and difficulty for a group of students and make cards from the key words from the text.

Before reading the text, put the students into pairs or small groups and allow them to put the cards in alphabetical order. This will make finding the cards easier as they are listening.

Alternatively, as a prelistening task, you could ask the students to predict the order in which the words on the cards will appear in the text.

As you read the text, the students grab the cards as they hear them; the winner is the student who grabs the most cards.

I think we can agree that this is an enjoyable activity. It can be used on its own in order to revisit a listening that the students have heard before, to review vocabulary from a listening (for example, you could make cards from all of the adjectives or verbs from a listening from a course book), or just as an opportunity for the students to practise and develop their listening skills.

As a possible extension, if you wanted the students to produce the text themselves, you could read the text again and have the students put the cards back into the correct order, then the students can use the cards to tell the text to each other in their groups.

From a teacher's perspective, a text grab is easy to prepare, productive, and students will find it fun.

....

Vocabulary Noughts and Crosses

Kristen Sharma

Levels	**Beginning to advanced**
Aims	**Recycle vocabulary in use**
	Focus on correct grammar and collocations
Class Time	**20 minutes**
Preparation Time	**2 minutes**
Resources	**Whiteboard**
	Nine target words

This activity is a good way to revise productive use of vocabulary, with a focus on grammatical accuracy.

PROCEDURE

1. Draw a large Noughts and Crosses (Tic-Tac-Toe) grid on the whiteboard.

2. Have students close all vocabulary books and dictionaries.

3. Divide the class into two teams. Have each team decide on a symbol that represents their team for use during the game. The symbol gets used on the Tic-Tac-Toe grid when a team wins a section.

4. Write the nine target words in the different sections of the grid. The words can come from a weekly vocabulary list or from a text students have been working on or are going to work on. Here is an example of words from a game in my classroom: *despite, fluctuate, integral, justify, predominant, reinforce, status, undertake,* and *valid.*

5. Tell students which team will start. Explain the rules of the game.

6. Both teams get 2 minutes to choose a word from the grid and to put together a perfect sentence using that word.

7. After the 2 minutes, the starting team has 20 seconds (or longer if you have less proficient students) to write their sentence on the board. They cannot

take up a piece of paper with the sentence written on it. During the 20 seconds, their teammates may call out if they see any spelling or grammatical errors.

8. Check the sentence. If it is correct, erase that word from the grid and put the team's symbol there. If it is incorrect, provide the appropriate feedback or elicit from the whole class what might be incorrect.

9. The second team then chooses a word and has 20 seconds to write a correct sentence on the board using it. They will usually choose a word next to the other team's symbol in order to block them. Ensure that different people on the two teams have a chance to write the sentences on the board.

10. The winning team is the first to get three of their symbols (i.e., three correct sentences) in a row, per a normal Noughts and Crosses game.

CAVEATS AND OPTIONS

1. Adjust difficulty by adjusting the level of words or the time constraints.

2. Get the student who wrote the sentence to then read it aloud in order to get the correct pronunciation of the target items, too.

3. If the class is too big to be divided into two groups, then it can be divided into four groups with two games running concurrently. The two grids would not have to have the same words on them.

Write It Right!

Marlise Horst, Joanna White, and Philippa Bell

Levels	High beginning
Aims	Raise awareness of homophones
Class Time	10 minutes
Preparation Time	2 minutes
Resources	List of 20 words
	Small whiteboards or slates
	Markers

PROCEDURE

1. Form teams of four or five students and distribute one whiteboard per team. Tell students that you are going to dictate some words (which should be a mixture of homophones—see Appendix—and other nonhomophone vocabulary studied previously by the class) for them to spell and that some of the words can be spelled two ways, for example, *see* and *sea*.

2. When you call out a word, their task is to consult quietly with their team. One of the group members writes the word on the whiteboard. If they know more than one way to spell the word, they should write it both ways.

3. When every team has finished writing, signal that they should hold up the boards for all to see.

4. Award points for correct answers if you wish to make it a competition—extra points for both spellings of the homophones.

5. Proceed in the same way for each of the words on your list. As you go, write the homophone pairs clearly on the board.

6. At the end, discuss what the homophones mean and their parts of speech. If you and the students speak the same first language, elicit the translation equivalents.

CAVEATS AND OPTIONS

1. If students know the same first language, you can elicit and discuss examples of homophones in that language. This raises linguistic awareness generally and makes the point that English is not the only language that has this "problem."

2. To expand, students can write silly sentences that use both members of the homophone pairs. Here are some examples:

   I want to <u>be</u> a <u>bee</u> and eat honey all day.

   Buy some shoes for the <u>bear</u> with <u>bare</u> feet.

3. Remind them to <u>write</u> the sentences <u>right</u>!

REFERENCES AND FURTHER READING

Beretta, A., Fiorentino, R., & Poeppel, D. (2005). The effects of homonymy and polysemy on lexical access: An MEG study. *Cognitive Brain Research, 24,* 57–65.

Cobb, T. (2013). Frequency 2.0: Incorporating homoforms and multiword units into pedagogical frequency lists. In C. Bardel, C. Lindqvist, & B. Laufer (Eds.), *L2 vocabulary acquisition, knowledge and use: New perspectives on assessment and corpus analysis* (Eurosla Monographs Series 2; pp. 70–108). Retrieved from http://www.eurosla.org/monographs/EM02/EM02home.php

Wang, K., & Nation, P. (2004). Word meaning in academic English: Homography in the Academic Word List. *Applied Linguistics, 25,* 291–314. doi:10.1093/applin/25.3.291

APPENDIX: *List of Some Common English Homophones*

hi/high	sent/cent	may/May
I/eye	fair/fare	road/rode
hole/whole	no/know	buy/by/bye
see/sea	new/knew	would/wood
hear/here	won/one	there/they're/their
meet/meat	two/to/too	read/red
right/write	bear/bare	would/wood
male/mail	beat/beet	so/sew
week/weak	ate/eight	way/weigh
blue/blew		

Recycling and Reviewing Classroom Vocabulary

Moira Taylor

Levels	*Beginner*
Aims	*Recycle and review classroom vocabulary*
Class Time	*15–20 minutes*
Preparation Time	*15 minutes*
Resources	*Classroom vocabulary that has already been introduced*
	Color 3x5 index cards; enough for half the class to have one
	Classroom control language (see Appendix)
	Alphabet chart (for reference)

This activity can be done any time after you have introduced new vocabulary that you want students to review. To succeed at this activity, students must have some facility with classroom control language and with the alphabet.

PROCEDURE

1. Choose up to 10 words that have already been introduced in your class. Prepare a set of index cards with the vocabulary you have chosen, following the model in Step 4. Make enough cards for half the class to have one card.

2. Tell students they will be reviewing some vocabulary. Prepare them by reviewing this dialogue:

    How do you spell_____? (A)

    It is _ _ _ _. Is that correct? (B)

    Yes, it is./No, it is not (isn't). Try again. (A)

3. Practice the dialogue as a large group. Then ask students to practice with their neighbor.

4. Show students the vocabulary cards you have prepared. On the sample cards below are nine common beginner-level words. Each card has only four or five words from the original list. The order is different on each card so that students are practicing all of the words, rather than repeating them each time they meet a new partner.

| listen |
| speak |
| write |
| correct |

| question |
| yes |
| answer |
| name |

| begin |
| listen |
| speak |
| write |

5. Ask for a student volunteer, and stand face to face with that student. Show the class that you have an index card with vocabulary, but your partner does not. Model that your partner should not see your card. Using the dialogue, ask the volunteer to spell the first word (e.g., "How do you spell *listen*?"). The student volunteer spells the word and then asks, "Is that correct?"

6. After modeling, set students up in two lines facing each other—one side with index cards to ask the questions about spelling, the other side without cards, but prepared to answer questions about spelling.

7. Give students about 2 minutes with their first partner. To switch partners, ask students with index cards to raise their hands. Ask the person at the end of the row of students with index cards only—not both rows—to walk all the way to the top of the line. She or he will now be face to face with a new partner. All the other students in that line should move down to face a new partner.

8. Do this three times, then ask students with index cards to give them to the students without index cards. Let them practice for a few more rounds in the switched roles.

CAVEATS AND OPTIONS

1. Create a new dialogue for students to practice pronunciation ("How do you pronounce #1?") or practice word meaning ("What does ____ mean?").

2. Do this activity weekly or daily. Use different-color index cards each week so that you can keep track of the vocabulary from week to week.

3. Have students make their own vocabulary index cards based on what they want to practice.

REFERENCES AND FURTHER READING

Allen, V. F. (1983). *Techniques in teaching vocabulary.* New York, NY: Oxford University Press.

Beck, I. L., McKeown, M., & Kucan, L. (2002). *Bringing words to life.* New York, NY: Guilford Press.

Nation, I. S. P. (2001). *Learning vocabulary in another language.* Cambridge, England: Cambridge University Press.

Zimmerman, C. B. (2009). *Word knowledge.* New York, NY: Oxford University Press.

APPENDIX: *Classroom Control Language*

Repeat that please.

I don't understand.

What does _____ mean?

Please speak English.

How do you spell _____?

Is that correct?

- Yes, it is.

- No, it isn't.

Accuracy Vocabulary Party

Natalia Petersen

Levels	*All*
Aims	*Consolidate accurate use of target vocabulary in context*
Class Time	*15 minutes+*
Preparation Time	*5 minutes*
Resources	*List of target words*

This game requires previous study of the target words. It is a good way for students to produce the target words in context, focussing on form.

PROCEDURE

1. Allocate a word to each student in the class from the list of target words.

2. Ask students to write a question using the target word which they can ask their classmates. Family words are fine.

3. Check the questions for accuracy before giving students a slip of paper to write their question on.

4. Once all students have a slip with a question, ask them to bring the slips to the front of the room and place them face down on a table.

5. Ask students to take a slip each, look at the question, memorise it and hide the slip behind their back.

6. Students then have a "vocabulary party," mixing and mingling, taking turns to ask and answer questions.

7. After students have asked a partner their question, they take another question and follow the same procedure, finding new partners to ask.

8. Conclude the task by asking students if they can remember any of the questions.

CAVEATS AND OPTIONS

1. Prepare the questions on the slips before class. This ensures students have good models to memorise.

2. Slips can be saved and reused with a focus on developing fluency so that students rely less on the slips and are given less time to ask and answer with each repetition.

Vocabulary Sorting According to Pronunciation

Laney Stephenson Pilhar

Levels	*All*
Aims	*Develop awareness of pronunciation of vocabulary items*
Class Time	*15 minutes*
Preparation Time	*15 minutes*
Resources	*Envelopes of 20–25 vocabulary items, each on a strip of paper for each group*

Each pair or group of three students will need an envelope with 20–25 vocabulary items, each on a strip of paper. The vocabulary items should be able to be sorted into two to five pronunciation categories. The categories could be based on consonant or vowel sounds, how many syllables the words have, or where the word stress falls. For example, if all of the words are plural nouns, you could give the categories "Ends in /s/," "Ends in /z/," and "Other." It is easier to first decide on the categories and then find words to go into each category.

PROCEDURE

1. Divide the class into pairs or groups of three, and give each group an envelope containing the vocabulary items (on small strips of paper) and the two to five categories (on larger or colored strips of paper).

2. Have students work together to sort the words into the correct categories.

3. Finally, check answers and drill pronunciation.

CAVEATS AND OPTIONS

1. To save on preparation time or in larger classes, vocabulary items can be written on the board and copied by students onto a list.

2. As an extension, students can think of additional words to add to each category.

3. The strips of paper can be used again and again for review activities, such as chain stories or writing assignments.

The Flyswatter Scanning Game

James M. Perren

Levels	*Beginning, high beginning, intermediate*
Aims	*Practice using active reading strategies for vocabulary development*
Class Time	*10–15 minutes*
Preparation Time	*5 minutes*
Resources	*15–20 target vocabulary items*
	Several clean, different-colored flyswatters
	Tape (easily removable) to mark a start line on floor
	Whiteboard marker or chalk

This an excellent pedagogical microstrategy for vocabulary review.

PROCEDURE

1. Prior to starting the game, provide a list of vocabulary words on the large whiteboard or chalkboard. (An alternative is to project the target vocabulary on an overhead screen.)

2. Create teams with an approximately equal number of students in each team depending on the number of students in the class and the amount of time available. For example, if there are 10 students, divide the class into two teams and have one student from each team come to the front. Guide the remaining students to form a line behind their teammate.

3. Use a different-colored flyswatter for each team.

4. Draw a dividing line with a marker or chalk from the top to the bottom of the board approximately at the halfway mark.

5. Explain the rules and give each teammate a clean and unused flyswatter.

6. Create a line on the floor using tape, up to 2 meters from the board. Each competing team member must stay behind the line until the announcer is finished saying the definition. Remind students that there is to be no pushing or shoving.

7. Each consecutive point winner must select and announce a word from the opposite side of the board from her or his own team to facilitate fairness in the competition.

8. The opposing players must keep their flyswatter on the board to see who landed first in disputed points (it is easy to distinguish the colored flyswatters).

9. Everyone on the team must swat, announce words, and repeat.

10. Teammates can help the active players locate the word by using whatever combination of languages and classroom management practices you deem appropriate.

11. No additional physical teammate assistance is allowed; in other words, a teammate cannot go to the board and point out the word for the player.

12. Briefly ask what the term is for *flyswatter* without using the actual word. Then write it on the board.

13. Provide the definition for a word. The student who swats the correct word receives one point for her or his team. Continue the game until every team member has gone and all the words have been chosen. The winning team receives a prize such as candy.

CAVEATS AND OPTIONS

1. Have students write the list of words on the board for a specific chapter. Continue this task if there are multiple chapters to review.

2. This activity can also include the use of other types of vocabulary, such as phrasal verbs, or different grammatical features of language, such as phrases, clauses, and sentences.

3. The game can be continued depending on how much fun students are having and how much time is available.

REFERENCES AND FURTHER READING

Gardner, H. (2006). *Multiple intelligences: New horizons in theory and practice.* New York, NY: Basic Books.

Krashen, S. D. (1982). *Principles and practice in second language acquisition.* Oxford, England: Pergamon Press. Retrieved from http://www.sdkrashen.com/content/books/principles_and_practice.pdf

Kumaravadivelu, B. (2003) *Beyond methods: Macrostrategies for language teaching.* Cambridge, England: Cambridge University Press.

APPENDIX: *Sample Handout for the Lesson*

Vocabulary Review Flyswatter Scanning Game Rules

1. Each competing team member must stay behind the line until the announcer is finished saying the definition.

2. No pushing or shoving.

3. Each consecutive point winner must select and announce a word from the opposite side of the board from her or his own team to facilitate fairness in the competition.

4. The opposing players must keep their flyswatter on the board to see who landed first in disputed points (it is easy to distinguish the colored flyswatters).

5. Everyone on the team must swat, announce words, and repeat.

6. Teammates can help the active players locate the word by using whatever combination of languages and classroom management practices the teacher says are appropriate.

7. No additional physical teammate assistance is allowed; in other words, a teammate cannot go to the board and point out the word for the player.

Vocabulary Deepening:
From Literal to Metaphorical

Jannie van Hees

Levels	*Intermediate to advanced*
Aims	*Expand word knowledge*
Class Time	*20–30 minutes*
Preparation Time	*30 minutes*
Resources	*Topic-related images*
	Recording sheets
	Display board
	Data projector

This activity expands students' word knowledge by focusing on the word's core underlying meaning and transferability to understand its family members. Students connect literal knowledge of the word to its metaphorical usage and meaning, thereby deepening overall word knowledge.

PROCEDURE

1. Select and introduce a target vocabulary item. The item may be one directly related to a topic in hand or one that learners identify that arises in class or which you think is worthy of attention.

2. Using the visuals to support understanding of the target word, develop a concise and precise explanation of the target word *hand*, first with students thinking on their own, followed by pair and group sharing.

3. Learners share the spoken and written form of the target word in their own language(s).

4. Scaffold learners' contribution to develop a consensus explanation; focus on the word's underlying meaning, which is the core meaning of the word and its family members.

5. Have students use a range of dictionaries to look up the word and compare explanations.

6. Students should develop fluency expressing the word, the consensus explanation, and word usage in contextually relevant sentences. Here is an example using the target word *hand*:

   - *the end part of a person's arm from the wrist, made up of the palm, four fingers, and one thumb*

   - *the grasping appendage at the end of a person's arm used for picking up and holding things*

7. After the collocation session, allow some time for learners to record any notes on the vocabulary from this exercise so they can review it another time.

8. Identify the word family members of the target word. Have students say and write down each word family member.

9. Share the list of word family members as a class by taking turns to nominate one. Each nomination should include

   - writing up the word for all to view,

   - pronouncing the word,

   - explaining the word,

   - using the word in relevant contextual sentences.

   e.g., hands, handy, handed, handless, handle, handful, unhand (me)

10. Scaffold for fullness of meaning-making and fluency, each time discussing the link to the underlying meaning. If learners cannot nominate many word family members, you can offer some examples.

11. Have learners work in pairs to identify phrases or expressions they may know or have heard or read using the target word.

12. Encourage them to share what they know as a class, making contributions yourself also, and compile a list of phrases and expressions. With a list of about 10 phrases and expressions, discuss the meaning, especially identifying how the underlying meaning of the target word informs the meaning of the phrase or expression, for example:

    lay a hand on something, hand in glove, go hand in hand, hand over fist, have a hand in something, be in someone else's hand, to hand over, out of hand, turn your hand to something, out of hand, a hand-to-mouth existence, to be handed something on a plate, to keep your hands off, to have time on your hands, a bird in the hand is worth two in the bush

13. Explain to learners that some are closely related to the underlying meaning while others seem not to be more or less congruent, more or less literal, more or less metaphorical. Explain and discuss the meaning of *literal, congruent*, and *metaphorical*. A simple way to explain these is as follows:

    • *Literal* means the obvious or most commonly known meaning.

    • *Congruent* means what the word is close to, the core underlying meaning of the word.

    • *Metaphorical* is not the obvious meaning (as in literal) but a somewhat hidden (nonliteral) or less known meaning.

14. Create a metaphorical continuum:

    Most LITERAL ——————————→ Least LITERAL

    Most CONGRUENT ——————————→ Least CONGRUENT

15. Ask learners to decide in pairs where each phrase and expression might be placed along the continuum. When sharing, they should be ready to justify their decision to the class.

16. Fully discuss each as a class—meaning, usage, and placement.

17. Develop little scenarios or anecdotes linked to each phrase, in pairs, as a class, or teacher provided, for example:

    He was nearly 80 years old and quite fit for his age. In former years he'd been a leading-edge scientist—a biologist, in fact. After retirement he said to his family, "I'm starting my own fish farm. I've got time on my hands now and I want to keep my hand in the area of biology I love best—fish hatching and fish preservation."

    She was always nervous when she stepped onto a plane. While she knew her safety and getting to the destination was in the hands of a fully trained, experienced pilot, she found it hard to relax. There was, of course, no other choice. Flying as a passenger went hand in hand with letting go and placing her trust in the flying crew.

18. Learners might choose or be given a phrase for which to develop a contextually relevant anecdote or scenario both in speaking and in writing.

CAVEATS AND OPTIONS

1. This approach lends itself more to some words than others. Be selective, particularly focusing on ones that arise in the classroom.

2. You may need to lead the way more or less, depending on learners' language proficiency.

3. As much as possible, give space for learners to grapple with unpacking the meanings of the phrases and expressions and be fully involved orally.

REFERENCES AND FURTHER READING

Macmillan. (2009–2014). *Macmillan dictionary.* Retrieved from http://www.mac millandictionary.com

Simon-Vandenbergen, A., Taverniers, M., & Ravelli, L. J. (Eds.). (2003). *Grammatical metaphor: Views from systemic functional linguistics.* Amsterdam, Netherlands: John Benjamins.

Flowery Speech: Integrating the Visual With Its Denotation and Connotation

Jean Arnold

Levels	*Intermediate +*
Aims	*Produce a poster with vocabulary information correctly matched and artistically arranged*
	Produce vocabulary review materials
Class Time	*15–20 minutes total*
Preparation Time	*15 minutes*
Resources	*Poster paper*
	Pictures of flowers
	Slips of paper with flower name and associated meaning (e.g., red roses, beauty and love; sunflower, loyalty)
	Markers, pens, or colored pencils
	Glue stick
	Tape
	Ribbon, paper doilies, Valentine-related supplies (optional)
	Blue tack or heavy duty tape to hang the posters

Afun activity to do, especially around Valentine's Day, is to have a lesson on flowers and what they signify. This lesson teaches the names of flowers, the denotation, and the connotation, or what each flower symbolizes to English speakers (see the Appendix; the connotations may vary from one English-speaking culture to another). The level of the class will determine how much, if any, presentation is needed of the adjectives that are related to the symbolism of the various flowers.

PROCEDURE

1. Make enough sets of pictures and slips of paper so that small groups of three or four students can work together.

2. You can quickly find pictures of flowers by doing an image search online, putting all the pictures in a word file and printing it out in color, if possible.

3. Hand out sets of the pictures of each type of flower and a slip of paper with the name of the flower and what it signifies. See the Appendix for some examples.

4. Have students match the picture of the flower to the card with its name and the flower's significance. Also give each group a sheet of poster paper and markers, pens, or colored pencils; glue stick; tape; and if available, ribbon, paper doilies, and other Valentine-related supplies.

5. Let students use their electronic devices to find the meanings of words they are not sure of and/or to check the meanings of the flowers if they do not know.

6. Get each group to create an aesthetically pleasing poster with information on the flower and its connotation and denotation, within the specified time, 10 minutes or so. Make sure that students have correctly matched the picture with the words' connotation and denotation before they fasten the information to the poster paper.

7. Have students hang up their poster and then get students to vote for the best-looking poster, which is then hung in a position of honor at the front of the room.

CAVEATS AND OPTIONS

1. An interesting discussion that may spontaneously arise is about the differing meaning associated with flowers or colors in students' native culture.

2. Other holidays that have numerous symbols with associated meanings can be visually represented to help students learn more about holidays in various countries. Cultural symbols could also be covered (e.g., in the United States: Statue of Liberty—freedom; Pentagon—military; NASA—space exploration; American flag—nationhood; in Vietnam: Ho Chi Minh mausoleum—founding father; Temple of Literature—education; water puppets—folk traditions; ao dai—women's traditional clothing; Vietnamese flag—nationhood).

3. In classes of mixed nationalities, students could create posters depicting national icons of their countries and what they represent. This option could be assigned as an out-of-class project, with their final product presented in class.

APPENDIX: *List of Flowers*

I found the following list at http://dynamo.dictionary.com/232830/what-does-that-bouquet-really-mean-popular-flowers-and-what-they-symbolize.

red roses	beauty and love
yellow roses	friendship
pink roses	appreciation
white roses	purity
daisies	innocence
lilies	humility and sweetness
lilacs	new love
tulips	trust
sunflowers	loyalty
hydrangeas	understanding and compassion
peonies	bashfulness
carnations	fascination
irises	faith and wisdom
orchids	rare and delicate beauty
hyacinths	playfulness

Negotiated Word Lists

Helen Howarth

Levels	*Pre-intermediate+*
Aims	*Practice selecting the most valuable words to learn or revise*
	Consolidate previous learning
Class Time	*10 minutes*
Preparation Time	*10 minutes*

One way to learn vocabulary is to select a list of useful words for students to learn thoroughly every week. However, this list may contain words that are already very familiar to students. One way to avoid this problem, and therefore select the most suitable words to learn, is to negotiate a word list with students. This method enables some student choice and results in additional learning about all the words from the group discussion. This method can also be used periodically to revise previously learned vocabulary.

PROCEDURE

1. To create a final vocabulary list of 15 words, for example, start with about 30–40 words. This list could be from either a text to be studied or previous vocabulary lists to be revised.

2. Divide the words between three groups, and ask each group to select 6 words for the final class vocabulary list. These finalists are then written on the board, and the whole class decides on the final 15 for the week.

3. If students also have their own independent word lists, they can add to them any words they would like to learn that were not chosen by the class. They can then research and learn these words themselves in their usual way.

CAVEATS AND OPTIONS

1. Provide guidance about not putting similar-looking or -sounding words in the same list in order to avoid confusion or interference when learning the words. Also, putting words with opposite meanings in the same list should be avoided.

2. You can encourage students to include multiword units or phrases in their lists as well as single words.

A Low-Stakes Vocabulary Test

Kieran File

Levels	*Any*
Aims	*Monitor vocabulary learning of weekly word lists and aspects of word knowledge*
	Positively reinforce vocabulary learning
Class Time	*15–50 minutes*
Preparation Time	*5 minutes*
Resources	*Piece of blank paper*
	Student vocabulary learning notebooks/worksheets with words that they have studied throughout the week
	Student dictionaries
	PowerPoint slides with details of the vocabulary tasks (optional)

This activity describes how to provide an opportunity for pushed retrieval and elaboration of weekly word learning as a way to positively enforce vocabulary. This approach was developed as a way to test weekly vocabulary learning of deliberately studied words in a low-stakes and positively reinforcing way. Students choose 15 words that they did not know or did not use from a list of high-frequency vocabulary. They study these words throughout the week, dedicating deliberate attention to a variety of aspects of word knowledge, including stress, meaning, word family, collocation, and use. The tasks that make up this activity provide a challenging opportunity for retrieval and elaboration of their studied words.

PROCEDURE

Before Class

1. Choose several of the following tasks (the first one is obligatory), or develop your own tasks to add to the list.

    a. Write down all 15 of your words you studied this week.

    b. Can you add the stress to each word?

    c. What is the part of speech for each of your words?

    d. Which of your words have a positive meaning? Put a (+) mark next to words that can have a positive meaning.

    e. Which of your words have a negative meaning? Put a (–) mark next to words that can have a negative meaning.

    f. Can you list a synonym for 10 of your words?

    g. What family word members can you recall for each of your words?

    h. What is the part of speech for each of these family word members?

    i. List one collocation next to your word.

    j. Choose 5 words and write a sentence about yourself/a family member/ your country/[*add your own topic*].

Vocabulary task no. 1	Vocabulary task no. 2
On a piece of paper write all of your 15 words	Now add the stress Word: vocabulary • ● • • • vo | cab | u | la | ry
Vocabulary task no. 6	**Vocabulary task no. 11**
Can you come up with a synonym for 10 of your words?	Have you used any of these words this week? Tell your partner when and where.

k. Have you used any of these words this week? Tell your partner when and where.

l. Choose 5 words you haven't used this week and think about where and when you might use them.

m. Discuss with a partner what you are going to do over the weekend/what you did last weekend/what you want to do in the future/[*add your own topic*]. Try to use some of your words as you discuss.

n. Can you identify any word parts that your words have in common with each other or with other words you know?

In Class

2. To re-create test conditions, students should ensure their vocabulary study books/worksheets and dictionaries are put away and that they have a blank piece of paper.

3. Students should then do Task a from Step 1. This will test their ability to retrieve the words they learnt during the week as well as test spelling.

4. Once they have written as many as they can (and don't be alarmed if they cannot write many), get them to check their worksheets/notebooks for the words that they could not retrieve and add them to the piece of paper. They should also check the spelling of the words they did retrieve. Then ask them to hide their worksheets again and prepare for the next task.

5. Carry out the remaining tasks you have selected. See the PowerPoint slides below and consider selecting three to five slides for each week's test. Give students enough time to complete the task, and follow up each task by getting them to check their answers using their worksheets/notebooks or dictionaries. In the tasks where they need to speak with partners, students can provide feedback to the class or to other pairs.

6. After the last task, students should be given time to identify the words and/or aspects of words from their weekly list that they feel they did not know well and to set goals for learning these words further.

CAVEATS AND OPTIONS

1. The tasks listed in Step 1 are only some of the possibilities for testing word learning and knowledge of a word. You can develop other tasks that have a positive reinforcement on vocabulary learning, target various aspects of what it means to know a word, and provide opportunities for retrieval and elaboration.

2. While scores could be kept for some or all of the tasks, they are designed as more of a low-stakes option to vocabulary testing, one that can help students identify words that they may need to pay more attention to.

REFERENCES AND FURTHER READING

Nation, P. (2001). Knowing a word. In *Learning vocabulary in another language* (pp. 26–30). Cambridge, England: Cambridge University Press.

Vocabulary and the Four Strands

- **Meaning-Focused Output**
- **Meaning-Focused Input**
- **Language-Focused Instruction**
- **Fluency**

Part III: Vocabulary and the Four Strands

Nation's (2007) concept of the four strands of a vocabulary curriculum is a useful way of planning and analyzing the type and amount of vocabulary-focused work in a classroom and in a curriculum. The four strands include three meaning-focused strands where communication of meaning is the main focus: meaning-focused input (through reading and listening), meaning-focused output (through speaking and writing), and fluency. Nation argues that these three strands should be given 75% of the time, with the remaining 25% given to language-focused learning.

In this section, the activities are organized in this order: meaning-focused output (where learning is through writing and speaking), meaning-focused input (learning through reading and listening), language-focused learning (deliberate study of aspects of words such as how they are pronounced and spelled), and fluency development. The order of the strands in this section is not the important point. The important point is that the four strands are a helpful guide for deciding how a vocabulary-focused activity might fit into a classroom activity or curriculum in a principled way.

It is worth evaluating a classroom activity using the four strands and considering the activity in light of the wider curriculum to see whether the four strands are present and whether there is balance in the strands. Tweaking or refocusing an activity can help with balance and the four strands. For example, if you have lots of meaning-focused input and language-focused activities, you can look at them to see how you might include output and fluency in the activity as well. If you have lots of direct learning and teaching of vocabulary, how can you build in opportunities for learners to use this vocabulary in their speaking and writing and encounter it in their reading and listening? And then how can you make sure that they have opportunities for fluency? For example, one way to incorporate fluency practice in speaking is to have learners repeat a speaking activity with a partner from the class. (For more on applying the four strands, see Hirsh & Coxhead, 2009; Nation & Yamamoto, 2012.)

The Caveats and Options sections of the activities in this part give suggestions for ways to incorporate another strand. For example, in "Structured Retell," by Joshua Brook Antle, you can find out how to include fluency in this meaning-focused output activity. In Mike Misner's activity "Narrow Reading Vocabulary Posters," he draws on all four strands, starting with meaning-focused input with reading and then language-focused learning, through to opportunities for

III

meaning-focused output through speaking and writing (which become meaning-focused input for others in the class) and then fluency development through repeated opportunities to present posters to classmates and discuss them. Note that while there are more activities in this part on meaning-focused output than on the other strands, this imbalance is just because of the number of submissions received that fitted into this strand.

REFERENCES

Hirsh, D., & Coxhead, A. (2009). Ten ways of focusing on science-specific vocabulary in EAP. *English Australia Journal, 25*(1), 5–16.

Nation, I. S. P. (2007). The four strands. *Innovation in Language Learning and Teaching, 1*(1), 2–13. doi:10.2167/illt039.0

Nation, I. S. P., & Yamamoto, A. (2012). Applying the four strands. *International Journal of Innovation in English Language Teaching and Research, 1*(2), 167–181.

Summarizing With Target Vocabulary

Jeff Popko

Levels	Intermediate to advanced
Aims	Encourage retention of new vocabulary
Class Time	15 minutes
Preparation Time	30 minutes
Resources	Class reading text at the appropriate level
	Online vocabulary analyzer (see References and Further Reading)

PROCEDURE

1. Choose a text of about 1,500–3,000 words that students have read (either in class or as homework). Create a text file (.txt) of the reading. Texts that are hard copy can be scanned into .txt files. PDFs can be turned into texts using Acrobat Pro software. Other electronic formats can be copied and pasted into a word-processing document or pasted directly into the analysis software.

2. Upload the text into the vocabulary analyzer and create an analysis file. Lextutor will give you a readout that shows how many of the words in the reading are also on the target vocabulary list, in this case the Billuroğlu and Neufeld list (BNL; Neufeld & Billuroğlu, 2006).

3. Choose a set of 12–15 words from the output to use in class. For example, in a graduate academic reading course that targets Level 5 of the BNL, the required textbook is *Annual Editions: Global Issues 13/14* (Jackson, 2013). The first reading is an executive summary of the textbook. An analysis of the text provided 65 word families from BNL Level 5, which can be divided into five groups of 13 words each (see the Appendix).

4. Randomly divide the lists into roughly equal subsets of words, and print the word lists for students to use in class.

5. Divide the class into groups, with each group receiving one list.

6. Ask students to write a summary of the chosen text using words from their list.

7. Have students highlight their target words in their summaries.

8. Post the summaries on a cork board (or online on the course web page).

9. Ask students to read their peers' summaries as follow-up. Students might highlight words from the vocabulary list.

10. Students could then use the summaries to study for the vocabulary quiz, which would take place the following week.

CAVEATS AND OPTIONS

1. Note that this activity is connected to a vocabulary list that has been chosen for a given group of students. In any reading there will be words that students don't know that are not on a given list, and lists will contain words that a given group of students already understand. The activity simply provides one way of embedding vocabulary study in a context.

2. The BNL list is convenient because of the online VocabProfile analysis software that can be used on Mac or PC. The BNL provides six levels of vocabulary difficulty.

3. The Academic Word List (Coxhead, 2000) headwords in the text can also be analyzed using the Corpus of Contemporary American English.

4. You can use words based on different curriculum targets, such as the Common Core (www.corestandards.org).

REFERENCES AND FURTHER READING

Compleat Lexical Tutor: http://www.lextutor.ca/vp/bnl

Corpus of Contemporary American English: http://corpus.byu.edu/coca

Coxhead, A. (2000). A new academic word list. *TESOL Quarterly, 34,* 213–238. doi:10.2307/3587951

Jackson, R. (Ed.). (2013). *Annual editions: Global issues* (29th ed.). New York, NY: McGraw-Hill Higher Education.

Neufeld, S., & Billuroğlu, A. (2006). *The bare necessities in Lexis: A new perspective on vocabulary profiling.* Retrieved from http://lextutor.ca/vp/bnl/BNL _Rationale.doc

APPENDIX: *BNL Word Families in the Text*

Group A	Group B	Group C	Group D	Group E
accommodate	acquire	adapt	albeit	aspect
assure	battery	category	centre	compute
concurrent	consequent	constrain	construct	convert
cooperate	cope	decade	derive	diminish
dominate	element	emerge	enhance	equip
expand	finance	fundamental	generate	highlight
ideology	illustrate	implicate	inevitable	infrastructure
intense	intrinsic	invest	locate	motive
norm	ongoing	outcome	overlap	participate
perceive	persist	precede	predict	proceed
reinforce	resource	ripe	scarce	scenario
secure	stable	strategy	sustain	transform
umbrella	undertake	vary	virtual	widespread

Structured Retell

Joshua Brook Antle

Levels	**High beginner+**
Aims	**Improve productive ability in using targeted words and phrases from readings**
Class Time	**10 minutes**
Preparation Time	**5 minutes**
Resources	**Breaking News English: www.breakingnewsenglish.com**

Reading activities can contribute to vocabulary growth, and retelling activities allows students to productively retrieve and make generative use of new words and phrases (Nation, 2001). This activity is best done as a postreading task.

PROCEDURE

1. Choose several new/difficult words or phrases from the text, and have students write them in their notebooks. Try to select words or phrases that will be essential for conveying the meaning of the passage. An example text and word/phrase list is included in the Appendix.

2. Divide the class into pairs.

3. Have one of the students in each pair retell the story while the other student listens. The first student must use all of the targeted words during the retell. Students are allowed to look at the targeted words in their notebooks while they are speaking.

4. Let the student who is listening give hints if the first student is having trouble.

5. Students then switch roles and repeat the activity.

CAVEATS AND OPTIONS

1. To increase the fluency demands of this activity, have students repeat the same retell three times as seen in a 4/3/2 activity (Nation, 2001). In a 4/3/2

activity, the student retells the same story three times to three different listeners. The speaker has 4 minutes to complete the first retell, 3 minutes for the second, and 2 minutes for the third.

2. To make this activity easier for lower-level students, choose a shorter text and allow students to write more words in their notebook (even words they are already familiar with). Conversely, this activity can be made more challenging by using a longer or higher-level text.

3. Another option is to have one partner retell the first half of the article and the other partner retell the second half.

REFERENCES AND FURTHER READING

Nation, P. (2001). *Learning vocabulary in another language*. Cambridge, England: Cambridge University Press.

Scientists find gene that erases memories. (September 25, 2013). Retrieved from http://www.breakingnewsenglish.com/1309/130925-post-traumatic-stress -disorder.html

APPENDIX: *Scientists Find Gene That Erases Memories*

Researchers from the Massachusetts Institute of Technology (MIT) have found the gene that could help people forget traumatic experiences. They say the research could benefit people with painful memories. Soldiers, crime victims and people who survived natural disasters are some of the people this research could help. Many of these people suffer from very bad stress because of their memories. It is an illness called post-traumatic stress disorder (PTSD). The scientists found the memory gene in mice. They hope that one day they can erase painful memories in humans. They think they can replace upsetting memories with more positive thoughts and feelings. This would help millions of people who suffer from PTSD.

Targeted words and phrases from the reading:

Gene

Traumatic experiences

Natural disasters

Suffer from

Post-traumatic stress disorder

Upsetting memories

Group Storytelling

Laney Stephenson Pilhar

Levels	*Pre-intermediate+*
Aims	*Use new vocabulary in creative writing*
Class Time	*30–40 minutes*
Preparation Time	*5 minutes*

PROCEDURE

1. Put students into a circle, and have each student take out a blank piece of paper to write on. They should write their names on the paper.

2. Select 10 lexical items and present them on the board. The vocabulary can be new, or it can be from previous lessons. It can make the stories more interesting if a couple of funny or exciting words are included in the vocabulary set (e.g., *to stink, poisonous snake, ambulance*).

3. Instruct students that they will be writing a story with their classmates using these words. Each student will start a story, but will be able to write for only 2 minutes before having to pass the paper to the person to his or her right. During each turn, students have to use one of the words from the list on the board. They should try to use different words each time.

4. Set a timer for 2 minutes, and allow students to start writing. When the time is up, students have to put down their pencils, even if they are in the middle of a sentence.

5. Next, each student should pass the paper to the student to his or her right. Then students read and continue the stories they have just received.

6. After five turns, the paper should be passed back to the student who originally started the story.

7. Give students enough time to read what their classmates have written, and instruct them that they now have to think of an ending for the story.

8. If there is enough time, students can volunteer to share their stories with the class. Feedback should focus on correct usage of the target vocabulary. Collect the stories in order to give feedback on common mistakes in the next lesson.

CAVEATS AND OPTIONS

1. To help students get started, you can provide an exciting first sentence on the board. Here is an example: *When John arrived at school, he noticed that all of the doors were locked and that no one was there. So he . . .*

2. When reviewing a large amount of vocabulary, each student can be given a different set of words to use in the activity.

3. This activity can also be combined with grammar practice for past tenses, especially if the vocabulary items are all verbs.

Deep Vocabulary

Mike Misner

Levels	**Beginner (young learner)**
Aims	**Quickly create sentences with target vocabulary items in the correct word order**
Class Time	**10–20 minutes**
Preparation Time	**20 minutes +**
Resources	**Page of word cards (Appendix A)**
	Word card placement sheet (Appendix B)
	One envelope per student

This activity helps students learn the form, meaning, and use of several sight vocabulary items. It also emphasizes correct word order.

PROCEDURE

1. Give each student an envelope and a sheet with a set of numbered target vocabulary items (Appendix A).

2. Have students cut out all of the target vocabulary items for the lesson and place them in the envelope. (Ideally, this would be done as homework the day before the class.)

3. Students should already know their numbers 1–100.

4. If students do not yet know how to read, call out the numbers for the desired words from the word card (e.g., 1, 9, 12, 18 = I am a boy).

5. Students place each word on the word card placement sheet (Appendix B) in the order that you call out, and read the sentence after you (e.g., I am a boy).

6. Call out several sentences, using words or numbers, according to the students' proficiency levels (e.g., She is a smart girl).

7. After students are accustomed to this activity, have them call out sentences for their partners, groups, or the class.

CAVEATS AND OPTIONS

1. Tell students that they are responsible for keeping their materials organized. If they lose something, they will have to re-prepare all of the lost materials again from scratch. This will mean much less work for you because students will be careful to not lose their materials. However, if some students do lose some items, they will spend their free time redoing all of their lost materials. Loss of free time is a powerful motivator for students to take care of their materials.

2. Have students race to see who can fill up the word card placement sheet with correctly worded sentences.

3. Have students make compound and complex sentences using *and*, *because*, and *which*.

4. Encourage students to tell a short story by connecting ideas across five sentences.

APPENDIX A: *Sample List of Word Cards*

I 1 L1 Translation	You 2 L1 Translation	He 3 L1 Translation	She 4 L1 Translation	We 5 L1 Translation
They 6	can 7	be 8	am 9	is 10
are 11	a 12	a 13	an 14	an 15
the 16	the 17	boy 18	girl 19	boys 20
girls 21	tall 22	short 23	smart 24	kind 25

Note: The words have to be much more salient than the numbers or translations for the students to learn from the cards and for them to more easily manipulate the cards.

APPENDIX B: *WORD CARD PLACEMENT SHEET*

1				
2				
3				
4				
5				

Pair Stories

Sonia Millett

Levels	*Beginning to intermediate*
Aims	*Recycle vocabulary in use*
Class Time	*30 minutes +*
Preparation Time	*10 minutes*
Resources	*List of target vocabulary*

This game is a good way to put target words into productive written use. It focuses on words in context and grammatical accuracy. Students choose words from the vocabulary they are currently studying in class.

PROCEDURE

1. Put students into pairs. Ensure that learners have different first languages if you can.

2. Tell them to clear off their tables, except for their vocabulary list and a pen.

3. Hand out one piece of A4 paper to each pair.

4. Display the following instructions on a whiteboard or screen.

> 1. Instructions
> 2. Write a story together.
> 3. Use 10 words from your list.
> 4. Write double space.
> 5. Highlight the words.
> 6. Don't use your dictionary.
> 7. Write a page.
> 8. You have 15 minutes.
> 9. When you are finished, check your work carefully.
> 10. Check again.
> 11. Bring your story to me to check.
> 12. Think about my feedback and revise your work.

5. After all the pairs have finished their stories and made efforts to revise, pairs can be put together to read or listen to other pairs' stories.

CAVEATS AND OPTIONS

1. Adjust the difficulty by specifying a topic (e.g., *Once upon a time there was . . .*).

2. Specify a tense—past or future.

3. Choose the 10 words.

4. Make sure the pairs are writing only one story. Negotiation is a major feature of the exercise.

5. Not being able to use a dictionary makes students use their own words. Dictionaries are useful at the final checking stages.

Target Vocabulary Use Through Meaningful Sentence Production

Wendy McFeely and Ulugbek Nurmukhamedov

Levels	*Intermediate +*
Aims	*Establish the fluency of target words through a productive activity*
Class Time	*5–20 minutes*
Preparation Time	*20 minutes*
Resources	*Voice recorders with playback*
	Timer or stopwatch
	Computer with speakers
	Software for assessing recording (e.g., Wavepad, Audacity)
	Prerecorded short text with target words (Appendix A)

Second language learners might recognize word peculiarities (e.g., spelling, definition, collocations), but word recognition does not guarantee word production. The focus of this activity is developing second language learners' productive vocabulary knowledge through the production of meaningful utterances.

PROCEDURE

1. Identify target vocabulary (e.g., academic, technical, topical words) for this activity. Keep in mind that a meaningful utterance is more than a definition. Instead of saying "<u>Feedback</u> means comments" or "<u>Feedback</u> means suggestions that can be used for the basis of improvement," students should produce an utterance (possibly longer than a sentence) that clearly demonstrates knowledge of the target word and ability to use it in a meaningful context. For example: "I like Ms. Smith because she gives me useful <u>feedback</u> on my writing. It's helpful in my final draft."

2. Organize practice activities, both collaborative and independent, to help students master meaningful utterances using the identified target vocabulary. When students discuss the target vocabulary collaboratively, facilitate these discussions by giving students information about target vocabulary (e.g., usage, collocations, idiomatic expressions) that can be used in forming meaningful utterances. Students should also practice meaningful utterances with the target vocabulary independently. Ample practice is necessary for students to master the use of target vocabulary in meaningful utterances.

3. After sufficient practice and feedback, tell learners that they are going to hear a prerecorded assessment for the target words in which they have to write down a meaningful utterance for each word. See Appendix A for an example. Tell them to be aware of the following points about the assessment task:

   • Different forms of the target word (e.g., expose: *expose, exposed, unexposed, exposures*) can be used.

   • One point is awarded for the correct meaning and clear use of the target word, zero points for no attempt or incorrect meaning and use.

   • Grammar is not assessed.

4. The prerecorded assessment can then be played.

CAVEATS AND OPTIONS

1. Choose assessment words from the practice target vocabulary.

2. For practice, assessment can be given orally (live). Students can work in pairs and then share their sentences with the class where sentences are discussed.

3. Students can use recorder-friendly cell phones to record sentences, listen to each other's output, and even email the audio file to you for feedback.

4. We have found that allowing students to write down ideas during preparation is not a good practice because it leads to students' reading prepared sentences into the recorder.

5. You can fill out grading/feedback sheets (see Appendix B) and return them to students.

REFERENCES AND FURTHER READING

Nation, I. S. P. (2008). *Teaching vocabulary: Strategies and techniques*. Boston, MA: Heinle/Cengage Learning.

APPENDIX A: *Prerecorded Test Script Example*

Turn on your recorder. Do not turn your recorder off until the end of the test (5 seconds). State your name (10 seconds). You will now hear five words. Each word will be read twice. After hearing the word twice, you will have 10 seconds to mentally prepare a meaningful sentence and then 20 seconds to record your sentence before the next word is read. Your sentence may contain a different form of the word provided. Only turn off your recorder when told to do so at the end. The test will begin now.

The first word is **theory, theory**. You have 10 seconds to prepare a meaningful sentence (10-second pause). You now have 20 seconds to state your sentence (20-second pause). The second word is **unique, unique**. You have 10 seconds to prepare a meaningful sentence (10-second pause). You now have 20 seconds to state your sentence (20-second pause). The third word is **factor, factor**. You have 10 seconds to prepare a meaningful sentence (10-second pause). You now have 20 seconds to state your sentence (20-second pause). The fourth word is **potential, potential**. You have 10 seconds to prepare a meaningful sentence (10-second pause). You now have 20 seconds to state your sentence (20-second pause). The fifth word is **praise, praise**. You have 10 seconds to prepare a meaningful sentence (10-second pause). You now have 20 seconds to state your sentence (20-second pause). This is the end of the test. Please push the "stop" button on your recorder at this time.

APPENDIX B: *Meaningful Sentence Grade Sheet*

Name: _____ Level/Section: _____

Circle the points for each item.

#	Word	Score		Teacher comment
1	theory	0	1	
2	unique	0	1	
3	factor	0	1	
4	potential	0	1	
5	praise	0	1	

Mid-Frequency Readers

Paul Nation

Levels	*Advanced*
Aims	*Bridge the gap between graded readers and authentic books*
Preparation Time	*5 minutes*
Class Time	*None*
Resources	*Selection of fiction and nonfiction mid-frequency readers*

This is not a class activity. It is a resource that you can offer to advanced students. Graded readers end at the 3,000-word level, but 9,000 words are needed for easy unsimplified reading. Use a selection of fiction and nonfiction mid-frequency readers that can be downloaded as free ebooks. The books are available at www.victoria.ac.nz/lals/about/staff/paul-nation. The mid-frequency readers are out-of-copyright texts, modified to three vocabulary levels (4,000, 6,000, and 8,000), and include, for example, the following titles: *Alice's Adventures in Wonderland, A Christmas Carol, Jane Eyre, The Art of War, More William, Free Culture, Metamorphosis,* and *Glimpses of Unfamiliar Japan.* If you would like to add to the growing list of titles by simplifying a book, please contact me at paul.nation@vuw.ac.nz.

PROCEDURE

1. Each learner works out his or her vocabulary level by taking the vocabulary size test at www.my.vocabularysize.com.

2. The learner chooses an interesting book at the most appropriate level and reads it. If the book is read on a Kindle reader or app, learners can easily look up unknown words. Ideally, learners at the 4,000-word level should be reading for a total of 2–3 hours a week.

3. Although the books are primarily for reading for pleasure, to increase the amount of vocabulary learning, learners could put the unknown words on cards as they meet them for deliberate learning. Because of the way the books are adapted, it is likely that all unknown words are useful for deliberate learning.

CAVEATS AND OPTIONS

1. The books involve only the replacement of low-frequency vocabulary, so there could still be grammatically based obstacles to reading. In addition, there may be issues related to background knowledge.

2. It is possible to read the same book again at different levels, as each book exists in three versions.

3. Learners' attitudes to mid-frequency readers and their effects on learning are as yet unresearched.

III

Narrow Reading Vocabulary Posters

Mike Misner

Levels	*Intermediate +*
Aims	*Gain expertise with the content and vocabulary on a topic of interest*
Class Time	*10 minutes*
Preparation Time	*2–4 weeks*
Resources	*Poster paper*
	Printed news stories
	Highlighters

Because students read vocabulary in context, make vocabulary lists, and present on the content using their target vocabulary items, this activity helps students develop deeper receptive and productive language abilities concentrated in an area of their chosen interest.

PROCEDURE

1. Have students select a topic that interests them, such as a popular issue (e.g., global warming) or a scandal (e.g., a cram school that leaked university entrance exam questions and answers to students before the test). Explain that they are going to be finding texts about that topic as a way to develop their understanding and vocabulary knowledge on it (for more on narrow reading, see Krashen, 2004).

2. Let students search the web to find four closely related articles (from the beginning to the end of a scandal or from different points of view on a topic). Ask them to bring the articles to class so you can check that they are on topic and appropriate for the student's language proficiency.

3. Ask students to read and highlight the words in the articles that they find difficult. They will establish individualized vocabulary study based on their own interests and needs.

4. Get them to make a vocabulary list (word + meaning + translation) from the highlighted words for each of the articles.

5. Have students create an original sentence in context for each difficult word. (This allows for deeper processing of the target language items than simple translation.)

   - X: The <u>tornado</u> was strong.

   - P: The 300 KPH winds of the <u>tornado</u> blew my house down.

6. Students then write a brief summary of each article using the target vocabulary if possible.

7. Have students affix the four articles, vocabulary lists, and summaries to a poster board which they will use to give a presentation.

8. In class on presentation day, place students in small groups in each corner of the class. One student from each group gives a 10-minute oral summary of the content of his or her narrow reading posters.

9. The small-group audience is responsible for asking at least two questions of the presenter about the content of the presentation.

10. Switch presenters.

11. Observe the multiple simultaneous presentations that are happening in each corner of the class.

12. Feedback can be given:

    a. Class: Always face your group, look at each member of your group, and speak loudly and confidently.

    b. Individual: I like the way that you connected all four stories.

    c. Rubric: Poster, organization, content, responses to group questions, pronunciation, gestures, body language, and so forth.

CAVEATS AND OPTIONS

1. Definitions, translations, and sentences which have little context can be copied and pasted from online dictionaries without much effort or learning. In order to be able to learn, students must make a sentence which is clear enough that their friends, who also do not know this word, can understand it from the context. If students demonstrate this ability, you will know that they made the effort to learn the target vocabulary.

2. Make virtual narrow reading posters on the class website, and require students to post questions and answers to each other. Then encourage the virtual reading poster to grow into something quite large.

3. Have a more advanced class present to a class of students with lower English proficiencies.

4. Have students use their notebooks/laptops and PowerPoint slides as posters. Then simultaneously project the presentations on the walls around the classroom.

REFERENCES AND FURTHER READING

Krashen, S. D. (2004). The case for narrow reading. *Language Magazine, 3*(5), 17–19. Retrieved from http://www.sdkrashen.com/content/articles/narrow .pdf

Make the Most of Dictations for Vocabulary Learning

Helen Howarth

Levels	*Intermediate +*
Aims	*Recognise vocabulary words aurally and spell them correctly*
	Consolidate understanding of the words' meanings
	Focus on the words in context, noting their grammatical form and collocations
	Practice pronunciation
Class Time	*10–40 minutes*
Preparation Time	*30 minutes*

Taking the time to prepare a dictation with the vocabulary words to be learnt pays off, as the dictation can be used for a multitude of activities. Ideally, the dictation will be 100 words and contain 10–15 of the target words. Try to use the words with good collocations. If the words come from a reading text, the easiest solution is to write a summary. Alternatively, the words could be used in a different context, unrelated to the original text. Be creative!

PROCEDURE

1. Students listen to the whole text to identify topic and main ideas.

2. Students listen again to chunks of the text and write what they hear on every second line in their books. As the dictation proceeds, increase the length of the chunks (e.g., up to 15 syllables) and the speed at which the chunks are read.

3. Students have 1 minute to check the accuracy of their work.

4. Students use a different-coloured pen to mark their work. Each correct word is worth one point. You may decide, however, just to mark the target word or collocations.

5. Scores can be kept by students or by you to monitor progress. If the dictation is 100 words, monitoring progress is easy.

6. Students should reflect on the cause of their errors and how to improve their accuracy in the future.

7. Have them listen to the text again to improve listening fluency and accuracy.

8. The dictation can now be used to discuss the words and how they are used, including the family words and collocations. The text can also be used for pronunciation practice.

9. If possible, record the dictation and make it available for students to further practise their listening, spelling, and speaking.

CAVEATS AND OPTIONS

For variety, you could try the following activities. They are in order of difficulty.

1. Prepare a gap-fill task sheet by blanking out the target words in the text.

   - Option A: Before distributing the sheets, have students listen to the dictation to identify the main ideas. Then hand out the sheets and have students listen again, filling in the gaps. Check their answers.

   - Option B: Include a word bank. First, students match the words to the gaps. This can be done in groups. Students then listen to the dictation to confirm their answers.

2. Create a split dictation. Students in Groups A and B have alternate sentences of the dictation which they read to each other while hiding their text. To enhance this activity, Group A can form one group and identify how to best chunk the dictation. You then practise the pronunciation with them, before moving on to do the same with Group B. Students from each group then pair up and do the dictation together. After they have completed the dictation, they use the texts to mark their work and then identify why errors occurred. Errors could be due to pronunciation or listening skills.

3. Use a running dictation. The dictation is in large print on a wall outside the classroom. A clear path to the dictation is prepared so students do not trip over anything. Students are in pairs or possibly threes. One student runs to the dictation and memorises a chunk. She or he runs back to the partner and recites the chunk, and the partner writes down what she or he hears. This continues until the dictation is complete. The partners can swap roles. You check the work and indicate how accurate it is, after which the students try to improve their accuracy further. The fastest, most accurate pair wins.

4. Have groups recreate the text. Instead of just marking the dictation, students form groups of three or four to rewrite the dictation together. They compare and use what they have already written to recreate an accurate text. The discussion and noticing of language forms that occur make this method very effective for language learning.

5. Incorporate a dictogloss (Wajnryb, 1990). Read the whole dictation twice without chunking. Students write down everything they hear or can recall. In groups of three or four, students recreate the dictation. A dictation of approximately 70 words is sufficient for this method.

6. Optional activities 3–5 lend themselves to some form of competition to be fast and accurate. Ask students what their accuracy goal is—95%? 100%? When they are ready to show their work to you, you should indicate how close to their goal they are and provide hints about what or where the errors are. Ideally, students will work them out themselves. The winning group is the first group to achieve their accuracy target. Other groups can refer to the winning group's dictation to check their own work if needed.

7. Make sure the ideas in the dictation are accessible or familiar to students. If both the ideas and the language are difficult, the task could be demotivating.

REFERENCES AND FURTHER READING

Wajnryb, R. (1990). *Grammar dictation*. Oxford, England: Oxford University Press.

Risky Business

Philippa Lyall

Levels	*All*
Aims	*Notice and correct vocabulary errors (family word or collocation) in writing*
	Explain accurate use of vocabulary in groups and to the class
Class Time	*20 minutes +*
Preparation Time	*10 minutes*
Resources	*Whiteboard*
	Pens
	Six sentences containing one or two vocabulary errors from students' writing

PROCEDURE

1. Divide the class into mixed-ability teams of three to four students.

2. Provide each team with a list of six sentences containing one or two vocabulary errors from their writing (one copy of the list of sentences for each team).

3. Assign a section of whiteboard to the teams for their answers and totals. Start each team with "$500" to bet with.

4. Ask the class, "Are these sentences correct?" Also mention that there may be one or two correct sentences.

5. Have the teams quietly study and discuss the first sentence for no more than 5 minutes. Then ask them to put their correction for the sentence on the whiteboard and decide how much of their money they are prepared to bet on whether their correction is right.

6. Invite one team with the correct answer to explain their correction(s) to the class. Confirm the answer and tell the team with the correct answer that they win what they bet; those with incorrect answers deduct their bet from their total of money.

7. Move onto the next sentence and continue as above.

8. The team with the most money at the end wins.

CAVEATS AND OPTIONS

1. Keep the pace quite fast and make sure everyone stops to listen carefully to the explanation of the correct answer given by their peers.

2. Teams can get quite competitive and noisy.

3. Include one correct sentence from a student's writing (anonymously) with a particularly nice feature you want the others to notice.

4. Teams can borrow from the bank to stay in the game if they have to.

5. The game can also be made more challenging with a grammar error as well.

Unpacking Vocabulary

Sasha Wajnryb

Levels	*Elementary+*
Aims	*Analyze new words to improve ability to remember and use vocabulary*
Class Time	*15 minutes*
Preparation Time	*None*

After using a text in an activity, students will have uncovered unknown vocabulary. This word families activity will focus on this new vocabulary. Ask students to choose five of these new words to focus on.

PROCEDURE

1. Write a table on the whiteboard with the following categories on the horizontal axis: *Word, Meaning, Translation, Pronunciation, Form, Word Family, Example.*

2. Choose one of the new pieces of vocabulary (e.g., *happiness*) and write it under the Word category.

3. Ask the class, "What does this word mean?" Write their answer (e.g., "feeling good") under Meaning. If students don't know the meaning, they should look it up in their dictionary. Encourage students to write the meaning in their own words, not copy a definition from their dictionary. Students can also write the word in their first language under Translation.

4. For Pronunciation, either write the word in phonemic script or ask students to write down how the word sounds phonetically.

5. Focus on the Form of the word and ask students what type of word it is and elicit the answer (e.g., noun) from the class. Add this information to the board.

6. Ask students to suggest other members of the word family (e.g., *happy, happily*) as well as their parts of speech (e.g., adjective, adverb). Write this on the board.

7. Have students now write their own sentences using the new word and/or word family in the Example category.

8. Finally, have students complete the table using their target vocabulary.

CAVEATS AND OPTIONS

1. For higher-level students, it is advisable to not use the Translation category. This will encourage them to use English to explore and learn new lexis rather than use their first language.

2. Recycling vocabulary helps students gain the confidence to produce new words. An intermediate step between learning and producing is practicing in a familiar context. Ask students to use their list of word families to write three to four sentences with each sentence using either the original word or one of the words in its word family. They should then erase or remove that word from each sentence. Keep a copy of these student-created sentences that each contain a missing word. After a few days, return to the sentences and ask students to complete the sentence using the word in the correct form. This recycling activity encourages students to learn all of the forms of the word.

REFERENCES AND FURTHER READING

Bauer, L., & Nation, P. (1993). Word families. *International Journal of Lexicography, 6*, 253–279.

Word-Family Focus

Amanda K. Ergun

Levels	All
Aims	**Build on vocabulary by learning different word forms and their functions**
	Use affixes as indicators to understand the various functions of words in sentences
	Establish foundational knowledge about word forms as a key tool for analysis of word function
Class Time	**20–30 minutes**
Preparation Time	**15–25 minutes**
Resources	**List of 5–10 vocabulary words**

The list of vocabulary words can be selected from either reading, grammar, or writing textbooks that are used by the language program or from the TOEFL or IELTS Academic Word Lists. These word lists can be obtained from older versions of the TOEFL or IELTS exams or from a generic Internet search.

PROCEDURE

1. Review sample sentences (either from the textbook or created in class) and discuss the function of each of the words. Then collectively discuss the role of affixes by analyzing vocabulary words and how these particular words change when prefixes or suffixes (or a combination of both) are added to the base word. Examples include but are not limited to the following: *happy* (*unhappy, happiness*), *help* (*helpful, unhelpful*), and *active* (*inactive, activity*). Note that the complexity of the sentences will reflect students' English proficiency level; for instance, beginners can easily analyze verb and adjective forms, whereas advanced students can analyze noun, verb, adjective, and adverb word forms.

2. Break students into smaller groups and have them work together to make (1) a list of 5–10 words that have both the base form and the changed form with the prefix and/or suffix and (2) a list of prefixes and suffixes with which

they are familiar. Words and affixes do not require specific order or listing, because they will be discussed in depth later. You can prompt students struggling with the task by suggesting that they list emotions to work with because of their various word forms.

3. Have students share and discuss words, their part of speech, and affixes.

4. From the students' lists, collectively sort the vocabulary words into the categories of noun, verb, adjective, and adverb. Have students identify the prevalent prefixes and suffixes based on these word forms.

5. As a class, work together to create the noun, verb, adjective, and adverb form of select vocabulary words. Examples include but are not limited to the following: *act* (*action, act, active, actively*), *discriminate* (*discrimination, discriminate, discriminative, discriminatively*), and *volunteer* (*volunteerism, volunteer, voluntary, voluntarily*).

6. Ask students to return to their groups and make sentences in which they use all the word forms of one of the chosen vocabulary words. For example, they will make four sentences in total by creating one sentence using the key word as a noun, another using the same word as a verb, a third using the word as an adjective, and a final sentence using the key word as an adverb.

7. You can provide feedback to students by focusing on the value of word form, function, and versatility and using it as a way to build a solid foundation of vocabulary for language development.

8. Discuss how the various word forms help students build their vocabulary and understand the function of different word forms in sentences. To enhance this reflection, again refer to the sample sentences. Stress the value of word forms and their unique functions in sentences. Again reiterate the fact that knowledge about word forms strengthens the foundation of vocabulary and expands a person's vocabulary.

CAVEATS AND OPTIONS

1. Potentially challenging with this activity is students' use of electronic dictionaries, as these dictionaries typically list outdated words or word forms that are uncommon. Another possible obstacle includes traditional perspective toward modern word forms. For instance, the word *globalize* is accepted as a common verb, but traditional perspective conflicts and asserts that this is not a common verb.

2. Ultimately, this activity can be adapted or modified by changing the reading selection (textbooks, periodicals, novels, pamphlets, etc.) or by transforming this activity into an editing task to make sure the words are used in the correct word form based on their function.

3. In order to focus more on word function, students can identify the part of speech for each word in a particular sentence and then analyze the function of all the words in the sentence and how they modify one another.

4. To help identify the word forms, students can read through an essay or journal article and search for the various word forms for select vocabulary words. Students will analyze the function of the word forms in the sentences, explain how they are used, and identify why they are different.

5. As a way for students to apply their knowledge about vocabulary, they can edit written materials to make sure that the correct word form is used according to its function.

Say a Synonym or an Antonym as Soon as Possible

Feifei Han

Levels	*All*
Aims	*Improve speed of lexical retrieval of known words*
Class Time	*10–20 minutes*
Preparation Time	*5–10 minutes*
Resources	*Selected words known to students*

F ast lexical retrieval is important in contributing to fluency in both spoken and written production (Snellings, van Gelderen, & de Glopper, 2002, 2004). Lexical retrieval refers to transforming concepts into linguistic codes (Kroll & Stewart, 1994; Levelt, Roelofs, & Meyer, 1999). It is the reverse process of lexical access, which is defined as accessing conceptual information through recognizing linguistic forms of a word (Snellings et al., 2002, 2004). This activity aims to strengthen students' existing vocabulary knowledge and to enhance the speed of lexical retrieval. Students may benefit from the improved lexical retrieval efficiency in their oral and written English.

PROCEDURE

1. Divide the class into pairs.

2. Give each pair two sets of the task materials. Each set includes a word list and a worksheet with answer keys. Each word list has 30 words with a variety of part of speech. Half of the words have a letter S next to them, and the other half have a letter A next to them (see the Appendix for a sample list).

3. In each pair, students take turns to complete the task: when they see a word with S, they have to say a synonym of that word as soon as possible. In contrast, when they see a word with A, they have to say an antonym of that word as quickly as possible.

4. The student who does not perform the task uses his or her watch or the classroom clock to keep a time record. At the same time, the student needs to use the answer keys to mark whether the answers are right or wrong by putting a ✓ for the correct answers and x for the inaccurate ones on the worksheet.

5. After finishing the task, students also write the time for task completion on the worksheet.

6. Each pair of students exchange the roles and repeat the above procedure.

7. Students then hand in the worksheets to you. You can use the worksheets as a record to make comparison among students or across multiple testing of each student to see if speed of lexical retrieval has been improved.

CAVEATS AND OPTIONS

1. This activity can be repeated regularly to check whether students have made progress in terms of speed of lexical retrieval.

2. This activity can also be used for written production. Students can write synonyms and antonyms on the worksheets, instead of saying them.

3. You can also introduce this activity for students to complete on their own after class as a way to improve their lexical retrieval speed.

REFERENCES AND FURTHER READING

Kroll, J. F., & Stewart, E. (1994). Category interference in translation and picture naming: Evidence for asymmetric connections between bilingual memory representations. *Journal of Memory and Language, 33,* 149–174. doi:10.1006/jmla.1994.1008

Levelt, W. J. M., Roelofs, A., & Meyer, A. S. (1999). A theory of lexical access in speech production. *Behavioral and Brain Sciences, 22,* 1–38.

Snellings, P., van Gelderen, A., & de Glopper, K. (2002). Lexical retrieval: An aspect of fluent second language production that can be enhanced. *Language Learning, 52,* 723–754. doi:10.1111/1467-9922.00202

Snellings, P., van Gelderen, A., & de Glopper, K. (2004). The effect of enhanced lexical retrieval on second language writing: A classroom experiment. *Applied Psycholinguistics, 25,* 175–200. doi:10.1017/S0142716404001092

APPENDIX: *Sample Word List and Worksheet*

Word List

You will see 30 words with either S or A next to them. You are required to say a synonym of a word as soon as possible when you see S and say an antonym of a word when you see A. The correctness of your answer will be noted by your partner, and the time of completion will also be recorded by your partner.

No.	Word	S or A
1	Near	S
2	Forget	A
3	Morning	A
4	Big	S
5	After	A
6	Look	S
7	Begin	S
8	Empty	A
9	Early	A
10	Rent	S
11	Immediately	S
12	Street	S
13	Arrive	A
14	Clean	A
15	Speak	S
16	Cheap	A
17	End	S
18	Weak	A
19	Lady	S
20	Ill	S
21	Same	A
22	Own	S
23	Good	A
24	Top	A
25	Ring	S
26	Small	S
27	Never	A
28	True	A
29	Difficult	S
30	Birth	A

Worksheet

Fill in the name of your partner first. Use your watch or the classroom clock to time the completion of the task for your partner. During the task, you also need to note the correctness of your partner's answers by placing a ✓ for each correct answer and X for each inaccurate one. Upon completion, fill in the completion time for your partner, and then hand the worksheet to the teacher.

Name: _____ Completion Time: _____

No.	Answer Key	✓ or x
1	Close	
2	Remember	
3	Evening	
4	Large	
5	Before	
6	See	
7	Start	
8	Full	
9	Late	
10	Hire	
11	Soon	
12	Road	
13	Leave	
14	Dirty	
15	Talk	
16	Expensive	
17	Finish	
18	Strong	
19	Woman	
20	Sick	
21	Different	
22	Possess	

23	Bad	
24	Bottom	
25	Call	
26	Little	
27	Always	
28	False	
29	Hard	
30	Death	

4/3/2 Collocation Pretask Activity

Joshua Brook Antle

Levels	*High beginner +*
Aims	*Improve productive ability in using targeted collocations*
Class Time	*30 minutes*
Preparation Time	*10 minutes*
Resources	*Online collocation dictionary: http://www.ozdic.com*
	Collocation dictionaries
	LTP Dictionary of Selected Collocations
	Oxford Collocations Dictionary for Students of English

PROCEDURE

1. Students complete a collocation worksheet similar to the example in the Appendix. The targeted collocations should be associated with a topic familiar to students. The topic will also be used for the 4/3/2 speaking task. In the example given below, the topic is pets, and the collocation worksheet asks students to prepare a list of several adjective, verb, and noun collocates for the noun *pet*. This activity prepares students to do the 4/3/2 speaking task (explained below).

2. Give students several minutes to complete the worksheet. Encourage them to use a collocation dictionary. Many electronic dictionaries have a collocation dictionary.

3. It is helpful to quickly check the answers as a class so students can add collocates to their lists. You can also use this step to discourage the use of unnatural word combinations.

4. Give students a few minutes to look over their collocation lists to make sure they understand all of the word combinations. Students can ask their partner or you for an explanation if needed.

5. Before starting the 4/3/2 speaking task, students choose their speaking topic. The topic should be connected to the collocation worksheet from Step 1. Here is the *pet* example:

Have you ever had a pet?

> If yes, tell your partner as much as you can about your pet. Try to talk for 4 minutes.
>
> If no, would you ever want a pet? Why or why not? Try to talk for 4 minutes.
>
> (Your partner can ask questions if you need help.)

6. Give students 1 or 2 minutes to look over the topic they choose to speak on so they can generate some ideas.

7. For the 4/3/2 task, students work in pairs. First, Student A discusses the topic for 4 minutes while student B listens.

8. Then they change partners. Student A now has 3 minutes to give the same talk to the new partner.

9. Partners then change again, and student A gives the same talk in 2 minutes.

10. Partner B then has the opportunity to discuss the topic three times.

CAVEATS AND OPTIONS

1. Speaking tasks, such as 4/3/2 (Nation, 2001), can be adapted to become vocabulary development activities (Nation, 2008).

2. The worksheet can be done as homework to save class time.

3. If students have trouble speaking for the full 4 minutes, allow their partners to ask questions to stimulate some new ideas.

4. It is better if students give their talk three times in a row as opposed to alternating.

REFERENCES AND FURTHER READING

Nation, P. (2001). *Learning vocabulary in another language*. Cambridge, England: Cambridge University Press.

Nation, P. (2008). *Teaching vocabulary: Strategies and techniques*. Boston, MA: Heinle/Cengage Learning.

APPENDIX

With a partner, find collocations for the word *pet*. You can also think of a specific pet such as a dog or cat.

Adjectives	Noun
	pet

Verbs	Noun
	pet

Noun	Noun
pet	

Possible worksheet answers:

Adjectives: domestic, family, house, household, beloved, abandoned, unwanted, lost, virtual, friendly.

Verbs: have, keep, own, allow, feed, bring in, let out, let in, take care of, train, walk (dog), give (pet) water, keep (pet) under control, mistreat.

Nouns: shop, store, cat, dog, rabbit, owner, sitter, food, hair, allergy, carrier.

No-Notes Speech

Julie Bytheway

Levels	*Intermediate to advanced*
Aims	*Develop fluent (automatic and fast) use of vocabulary*
Class Time	*10–60 minutes*
Preparation Time	*2 minutes*
Resources	*Small pieces of paper (big enough to write one word on)*
	Two papers for each learner that are visually different (e.g., white/yellow, lined/unlined)

Learners need low-stakes, enjoyable activities that include a sense of urgency to practice speaking vocabulary fluently. This activity uses learners' ideas and needs no preparation from the teacher, other than finding (ripping/cutting up) pieces of paper. Learners of different levels can do the activity alongside each other, adapting it to their own level and current learning needs.

PROCEDURE

1. Give every learner one small piece of paper.

2. Ask learners to write a profession on the paper. They can be as creative as they like (e.g., brain surgeon, pole dancer, goldfish whisperer).

3. Collect the papers.

4. Give every learner another (visually different) piece of paper.

5. Ask learners to write the name of a really famous person on the paper. The person can be dead or alive, real or fictional, but must be easily known (e.g., Donald Duck, Oprah Winfrey, Albert Einstein).

6. Collect the papers.

7. Shuffle the profession papers and shuffle the people papers.

8. Ask learners to choose an unknown paper from the profession pile and an unknown paper from the people papers.

9. Ask learners to plan three ideas why their person deserves a job in that profession. This planning can be done individually, in pairs, or in small groups and it can be logical, creative, or funny. Learners can speak in third person (e.g., Michael Jordan should be hired as a nurse because . . .) or first person (e.g., I am Mother Teresa and you should hire me as an electrician because . . .).

10. Ask learners to independently practice a 1-minute (more than 30 seconds and less than 90 seconds) speech to justify why their person deserves to have a job in that profession, which is supported with three reasons.

11. Ask learners to come back in 3 to 5 minutes.

12. Learners practice their speech aloud to themselves and do not write down any notes.

13. When learners return, ask them to share their speech, with either changing partners, a small group, or the whole class.

CAVEATS AND OPTIONS

1. Learners can share their speeches in different ways, with either changing partners, a small group, or the whole class.

2. High school students that are infrequently (high stakes) assessed from speeches in front of the whole class can use this activity as a (low stakes) opportunity to speak in front of the whole class.

3. IELTS and Cambridge exam candidates can use this activity as an opportunity to purposefully include a variety of vocabulary.

4. The two topics can be adapted: Instead of professions try hobbies or sports; instead of famous people try teaching staff or characters in book or film studied in class. At the end of the activity, ask learners to reflect on the activity. What was easy? What was hard? How was it "learnful"?

Strategies for Vocabulary Learning

- **Using Dictionaries**
- **Learning More About Words**
- **Developing Autonomy**

IV

Part IV: Strategies for Vocabulary Learning

Strategies for vocabulary learning are not isolated activities. They need to be integrated into the regular classroom and independent learning activities of the learners and practiced to develop fluency in their use. Learners need training and support to help them become familiar and fluent with strategies. We can divide strategies into categories such as direct and indirect (Coxhead, 2006). This distinction can help us see when we are directing learners toward deliberate word-learning strategies, including using word cards and studying word parts such as common affixes and suffixes. Indirect learning strategies include extensive reading, for example, when learners are focused on the message in the text, rather than consciously paying attention to directly learning the words that appear in the text.

The activities in this part of the book are divided into three main areas. The first section is on using dictionaries. Part of the recent innovations in dictionary making has been the development of collocation dictionaries for second and foreign language learners. These dictionaries can be found online or in printed book form, and they are important for finding out more about words as they appear in multiword units.

The second section is on learning more about words using strategies. One strategy which has stood the test of time is word cards (for more on this strategy, see Nation, 2013). In an interview from 2005, Paul Nation explained how he convinces learners (and teachers) of the power of direct learning techniques such as word cards:

> The best way to convince learners is to give them a little bit of instruction about how to do it and then make them do it. I do this with my MA students in my teaching and learning vocabulary course. They have to learn fifty words of the survival vocabulary in a language they don't know. They do it because they have to do an assessed task on it. The task requires them to keep a record of their learning of these words. It blows their mind. They discover that they can learn a lot in a very short time. It usually takes them longer to make the cards than to learn the words. Having done it and seen the spectacular rates of learning, they are well convinced. (quoted in Coxhead, 2005, p. 47)

Other strategies in this section aim for learners to build bridges using their first language, when possible, with vocabulary in their second language. For example, for speakers of Spanish, the word *parentheses* is much easier to remember than the synonym *brackets*, because of the connection between Spanish (*paréntesis*) and English. Strategies can cover a wide range of activity from learners, from focusing on different aspects of word knowledge through to drawing connections or relationships between words in new and novel ways to strengthen learning. For example, one activity in this section encourages learners to learn more about words using art.

The final section in this part is on developing autonomy. The purpose of this section is to draw attention to the need for learners to think about and use strategies outside the classroom for their vocabulary learning. This is done through techniques such as working with unknown words in context through to discussing and ranking strategies themselves as a way to bring the outside world in to the classroom and to raise awareness of strategy use for vocabulary learning. Through encouraging learners to talk about the strategies they use, evaluate their success, adapt them to suit new situations or new learning goals, and share their strategies with other students, we can help their development as independent learners.

REFERENCES

Coxhead, A. (2005). State of the Nation: An interview with Paul Nation. *RELC Guidelines, 27*(1), 46–50.

Coxhead, A. (2006). *Essentials of teaching academic vocabulary.* Boston, MA: Houghton Mifflin.

Nation, I. S. P. (2013). *Learning vocabulary in another language* (2nd ed.). Cambridge, England: Cambridge University Press.

Working With Collocation Dictionaries

Anna Siyanova-Chanturia

Levels	**Intermediate+**
Aims	**Learn about and work with collocation dictionaries**
	Gain awareness of collocations
Class Time	**5–10 minutes per activity**
Preparation Time	**10–20 minutes**
Resources	**Collocation dictionaries**

PROCEDURE

1. Introduce students to collocation dictionaries (see References and Further Reading). Explain that collocation dictionaries will help them find more accurate and more diverse ways of expressing ideas and thoughts.

2. Using a collocation dictionary, choose 5–10 common nouns and provide 5–6 verbs they often appear with. Then find another verb that does not collocate with the target noun (this verb should not be chosen randomly, but should, for example, be synonymous with one of the "good" verbs). Ask students to find the verb that does not collocate with the target noun. For example:

Noun	Choose Collocation From List	Answer Key
child	adopt, bear, grow, spoil, feed, nurse	grow
control	exercise, gain, establish, lose, assume, apply	apply
fight	pick, provoke, fail, lose, win, wage	fail
influence	exert, have, exercise, employ, consolidate, strengthen	employ
horse	mount, ride, walk, groom, coach, breed	coach
knowledge	acquire, reach, accumulate, gain, soak up, deepen	reach
office	accept, assume, seek, stand for, hold, take	accept

3. Students can first try guessing on their own and then use the dictionary to check their answers.

CAVEATS AND OPTIONS

1. The activity can be adjusted to other collocation types. See the Appendix for some more examples. Using your preferred collocation dictionary, prepare a list of adjectives, all of which collocate with the same noun, for 5–10 nouns. Then ask students to identify a noun that collocates with all the adjectives given. For example:

   a. awkward, embarrassing, irrelevant, complicated, rhetorical, tricky

      _____

   b. second, strong, right, helping, firm, weak _____

   c. substantial, strong, clear, reliable, material, forensic _____

   d. advanced, introductory, elective, intensive, postgraduate, intermediate

      _____

   e. supernatural, colonial, industrial, absolute, foreign, healing

      _____

   (answers: a = question, b = hand, c = evidence, d = course, e = power)

2. This activity can also be done in groups, with you awarding points for the right answers. For example, six points are awarded for the correct answer given after one word, five points after two words, four points after three words, and so on. You can read the words aloud, one by one, or gradually reveal them on the board. The group that gets most points wins.

3. Make sure to give learners plenty of opportunities to encounter these collocations in context and use them in their writing and speaking.

REFERENCES AND FURTHER READING

Benson, M., Benson, E., & Ilson, R. (Eds.). (1997). *The BBI dictionary of English word combinations.* Amsterdam, Netherlands: John Benjamins.

McIntosh, C., Francis, B., & Poole, R. (Eds.). (2009). *Oxford collocations dictionary for students of English.* Oxford, England: Oxford University Press.

Rundell, M. (Ed.). (2010). *Macmillan collocations dictionary.* Oxford, England: Macmillan Education.

APPENDIX: *Common Types of Collocations*

Verb + Noun Collocations

combat terrorism

restore peace

lose control

Some of the most common English verbs are *have, take, make, give,* and *do* (so-called delexical verbs). These verbs can be combined with many different nouns to form frequent verb + noun collocations.

Noun + Noun Collocations

These collocations are very common in English. In noun + noun collocations, the first noun defines the second. The second noun is called head noun. For example:

chocolate <u>bar</u>: a bar of chocolate

school <u>teacher</u>: a teacher at school

safety <u>belt</u>: a belt to use for personal safety

Adjective + Noun Collocations

strong tea

false accusations

physical activity

IV

Playing With a Picture Dictionary

Mike Misner

Levels	*Beginner and intermediate*
Aims	*Work with the vocabulary words within a semantic field*
Class Time	*10 minutes*
Preparation Time	*None*
Resources	*Picture dictionaries*

There are many possible word games that can be played with picture dictionaries.

PROCEDURE

Guess what I am thinking of?

1. Student A writes a word from the page of the picture dictionary on a piece of notebook paper and keeps the word a secret (e.g., *lawnmower*).

2. Student B guesses a word from the page (e.g., Is it a garden hose?).

3. If the guess is incorrect, Student A says "No" and gives a hint (e.g., It is a machine.).

4. This continues until Student B guesses correctly.

5. Student A shows the paper with the answer on it.

6. Students switch roles.

Guess where I am hiding?

1. Student A pretends to be a tiny animal or thing.

2. Student A writes her or his location on the picture dictionary page on a piece of notebook paper and keeps the location secret (e.g., I am under the lawnmower.).

3. Student B guesses a location on the page (e.g., Are you in the garden?).

4. If the guess is incorrect, Student A answers "No" and gives a hint (e.g., I am on the right side of the page.).

5. This continues until Student B guesses correctly.

6. Student A shows the paper with the answer on it.

7. Students switch roles.

I use a _____ to _____.

1. Student A chooses an item and makes a question (e.g., What do you use the garden hose for?).

2. Student B chooses a second item and makes an answer (e.g., I use a garden hose to water the flowers.).

3. Students take turns making questions and answers about the content of the page in the picture dictionary.

4. Students can elicit different answers by asking different types of questions (e.g., How often do you use the garden hose? Is the lawnmower noisy? What do you use to plant the garden?).

CAVEATS AND OPTIONS

1. There are many other possible options for games with the vocabulary in picture dictionaries. Use your teaching imagination (e.g., I spy, 20 questions, hangman, storytelling with several objects from the page, shopping for items on the page).

2. Instead of a picture dictionary, magazine or online pictures and an electronic or online dictionary can be used.

3. Photographic Dictionary (http://photographicdictionary.com) has a large number of good quality pictures with explanations in context.

IV

Collocation Look-Up Strategies for Second Language Writers

Ulugbek Nurmukhamedov

Levels	*Intermediate+*
Aims	*Develop online dictionary look-up strategies for productive collocation use in second language writing*
Class Time	*60 minutes (preferably four 15-minute sessions)*
Preparation Time	*10 minutes*
Resources	*Computers with Internet access*
	Worksheet (see Appendices A–D)

PROCEDURE

1. Teach students the definition of *collocation* (i.e., two or more words that co-occur), focusing on the following collocation types that are problematic for second language learners: verb + noun (e.g., *tackle problems, run a company*) and adjective + noun (e.g., *foreign language, wild guess*).

2. Introduce an online learner dictionary to students (see References and Further Reading).

3. Familiarize students with the following collocation look-up strategies: (a) pay attention to special collocation boxes because they list several collocations; (b) read example sentences because collocations are often **bolded** or *italicized* in example sentences.

4. See the appendices for exercises that are sequenced from easy to difficult, starting with words (Appendix A) and then moving to sentences (Appendix B), a short paragraph (Appendix C), and a longer paragraph (Appendix D).

5. Have students complete Appendices A and B, then lead a whole-class discussion about the collocation choices and their meanings.

6. Have students complete Appendices C and D, then lead a whole-class discussion to elaborate why certain collocations are acceptable but others are not.

CAVEATS AND OPTIONS

1. If there is no access to an online dictionary, you can use hard-copy learner dictionaries. Most learner dictionaries published after 2000 contain information about collocations.

2. You can choose to use any popular learner dictionary or decide on a special collocation dictionary such as the *Longman Collocations Dictionary and Thesaurus* (2014) or *Macmillan Collocation Dictionary for Learners of English* (2010).

3. You can demonstrate effective strategies for finding collocations in the *Longman Dictionary of Contemporary English* by sharing the following video tutorial: www.youtube.com/watch?v=11adY1wXB50.

REFERENCES AND FURTHER READING

Cambridge dictionaries online. (2014). Retrieved from http://dictionary.cambridge .org/us

Longman collocations dictionary and thesaurus. (2014). New York, NY: Pearson Longman.

Longman dictionary of contemporary English. (n.d.). Retrieved from http://www .ldoceonline.com

Macmillan collocations dictionary for learners of English. (2010). Oxford, England: Macmillan.

Macmillandictionary. (2009–2013). Retrieved from http://www.macmillandictionary .com/us

Walter, E., & Woodford, K. (2010). *Using collocations for natural English.* Peaslake, England: Delta ELT.

APPENDIX A: *Starting With Words*

Use the dictionary to find one verb and one adjective collocation for each noun. Write your choice(s) in the box.

Example:

Noun	Verb	Adjective
Language	speak a language	foreign language

Noun	Verb	Adjective
Task		
Company		
Money		

APPENDIX B: *Moving to Sentences*

Use the dictionary to fix the wrong collocation (**bolded**). Write the correct collocation inside the brackets.

Example: She **answers** her responsibility as a nurse very seriously.

[**answer**: takes]

1. I took pills for my headache but they didn't **solve** any effect.

[answer: _____]

2. Abdullah finds it easy to speak to **full** strangers.   [answer: _____]

3. I really do not know the answer, but I'll make a **modest** guess.

[answer: _____]

APPENDIX C: *A Short Paragraph*

Read the short paragraph below and use the dictionary to fix the wrong collocations (**bolded**). Write down your answers in the Revised Collocations column of the table.

I really wanted to work as a fashion journalist, thus I applied for jobs with different newspaper publishers. Finally, in 2004, I found a job as a fashion editor for a national newspaper. It was the job of my dreams and I worked hard. In order to (1) **organize** a deadline, sometimes I had to stay late. I did not mind the (2) **uneasy** work because at last I had (3) **built** my ambition.

	Wrong Collocations	Revised Collocations
1	organize a deadline	
2	uneasy work	
3	built ... ambition	

APPENDIX D: *A Longer Paragraph*

Alumni attending a school reunion were asked to write something about their school days and their lives since. There are six **bolded** wrong/awkward collocations (three verbs and three adjectives) in the paragraphs below. Use the dictionary to fix these problems. Write down your answers in the Revised Collocations column of the table. One example is provided for you.

My English teacher, Mrs. Evans, was (0) a prime figure in my education, and the main reason I went on to study English at the university. She made me realize that I needed to (1) **catch** a good education. Because of her, I made it my (2) **advanced** priority to do well on my exams. In her classes, we were encouraged to (3) **open** our opinions freely, and we discussed all the (4) **upper** issues of the day. She really opened our minds.

In college, I was lucky enough to have Professor Kim, a leading expert in English Literature. I have almost completed my degree, and am giving serious consideration to a career as a schoolteacher myself. Mrs. Evans and Professor Kim are the (5) **high** examples of the sort of teachers who (6) **create** an enormous influence on students' lives.

IV

	Wrong Collocations	Revised Collocations
0	**prime figure**	**key** figure
1	**catch** ... education	
2	**advanced priority**	
3	**open** ... opinions	
4	**upper** issues	
5	**high** examples	
6	**create** ... influence	

Spaced-Repetition Flashcards

Charles Browne

Levels	*All*
Aims	*Quickly and efficiently master a large number of high-frequency words*
Class Time	*Minimal*
Preparation Time	*Varies*
Resources	*Stack of index cards to make into flashcards*
	Plastic accordion file to hold the cards (need five sections)
	Access to a dictionary to help with definition writing

PROCEDURE

1. Print out a list of words and definitions you want students to master. You could have them work with a list of key words from the class text or a test they are preparing for. Or if you want to do something more comprehensive, you could download and use the New General Service List (Browne, 2013) and definitions (whose 2,800 words give students 90% coverage of most reading texts) at www.newgeneralservicelist.org.

2. Have students spend time going through the list and definitions, highlighting all the words they don't know or are not confident about.

3. Ask students to bring to the next class a large stack of white index cards and a small plastic accordion folder with at least five pockets.

4. Have students create flashcards for the first 100 words they have highlighted (in order of frequency).

5. Show students how to make a flashcard, putting the word in English on one side and filling the other side with whatever information you or they deem important, for example, definition, part of speech, sample sentence, common collocates, a picture or other mnemonic device to help them. Then give them some class time to begin working on their cards. Walk around the room to help, and allow students to work together, brainstorm, and learn from each other how to make good flashcards.

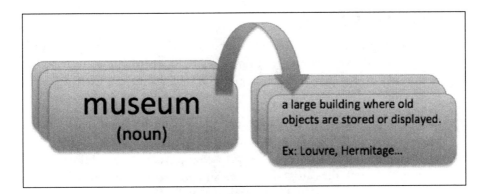

6. Briefly explain to students the principles of spaced learning: that reviewing the words several times at longer and longer intervals will greatly increase their ability to learn and remember new vocabulary. They should label each of the slots in their accordion file to match one of the intervals. There are several different recommended repetition intervals, but a good one is to label the five slots as follows: New Words, 24 hours, 3 days, 1 week, 3 weeks.

7. Instruct students to put their 100 word cards in the first slot, and as they study and get words correct, they put those cards in the next slot for review after the appropriate time has elapsed. Tell them that if they get a word incorrect at any time (even if it has moved to the third or fourth slot), they should put that card back to the first. This is a key principle of spaced repetition which ensures more study and review of problematic words.

8. Tell students that although their learning will be completely self-directed, the vocabulary quizzes (and their grades) will be decided by you as follows:

    a. You will set a goal of a specific number of words for students to learn per semester, usually in multiples of 100. If you say 500 words, then there will be five quizzes worth 100 points each.

    b. A quiz consists of a student handing you the stack of 100 words he or she has been studying and then you randomly selecting 10 out of the 100 and quizzing the student on them (6 out of 10 words correct = 60%, etc.).

    c. Students can take the quiz any time they like.

CAVEATS AND OPTIONS

1. If possible, set aside a few minutes each class for students to talk with each other and with you about any difficulties they are having as well as any techniques or tips they have come up with which they can exchange with each other.

2. Depending on the goals of the course, the students' "grade" can easily be more focused on motivating them to master their word lists rather than strict grading. For example, if they get a low score, you can allow them to go back and study the cards some more and then retake the quiz (the Kyoto program set 80% mastery of each stack as a goal).

REFERENCES AND FURTHER READING

Browne, C. (2013). The new general service list: Celebrating 60 years of vocabulary learning. *The Language Teacher*, *37*(4), 13–16.

Mondria, J.-A., & Mondria-De Vries, S. (1994). Efficiently memorizing words with the help of word cards and "hand computer": Theory and applications. *System*, *22*, 47–57. doi:10.1016/0346-251X(94)90039-6

The Art of Learning Vocabulary

Jean Arnold

Levels	Any
Aims	*Develop strategies for learning vocabulary*
	Analyze word usefulness
	Engage in artistic expression
	Create useful review materials
Class Time	*30–60 minutes*
Preparation Time	*30 minutes*
Resources	*Text(s) with vocabulary for students to commit to memory*
	Picture of a hanging mobile or a real one (see Appendix)
	Dictionary
	Art supplies

PROCEDURE

1. You can either give students texts and ask them to underline the 10 most important new words in it or give each group a list of 10–12 key words in a discipline, Academic Word List words (Coxhead, 2000), key vocabulary from a class textbook, and so on. If students are choosing their own words, have them read the text as homework and brainstorm which words are most important/useful.

2. Put students into groups of about four. In classes with a variety of speakers of different languages, I try to ensure that each group has a mix to make speaking English a necessity. Have students discuss with their teammates which words they are going to select to include in their mobile. See the Appendix for an example of a mobile. They have to give reasons why the words should or shouldn't be included. When they agree on their words, or if you give them the 10 or so words, explain that the next day they will be making a mobile that includes all these words.

3. Show an illustration of a mobile or a real one so they have an example of a final product.

4. Have students print a large-font copy of the words before the next class, send you a list of their words to print out ahead of time, or write the words on card stock in big letters the day of the project.

5. On the mobile-making day, give students art supplies such as string/thread, sticks, straws, pipe cleaners, paper clips, a hole punch, tape, thick paper or card stock, scissors, and colored pens.

6. Set a time limit (30–40 minutes), and have students work in their groups to decorate and/or illustrate the words they chose, arranging and balancing the words in the mobile, which will then be hung in the classroom.

7. Have students go around and look at the other groups' mobiles and discuss which they like best and why.

CAVEATS AND OPTIONS

1. If the student groups are working with different texts or chapters of their vocabulary books, they can create useful study materials for the rest of the class and learn useful methods to further their own vocabulary-building efforts. You can group words by vocabulary family.

2. If you show students various pictures of mobiles ahead of time, you might involve them in the collection of materials. It also helps if they can have a rough idea of how they're going to construct the mobile ahead of time.

3. This activity can also be an out-of-class extra credit project for students.

4. It helps to have a classroom with a low ceiling; if the ceilings are high, it gets tricky to hang the mobiles.

REFERENCES AND FURTHER READING

Coxhead, A. (2000). A new academic word list. *TESOL Quarterly, 34,* 213–238. doi:10.2307/3587951

APPENDIX: *Example of a Mobile*

Finding Friends

Marlise Horst, Joanna White, and Philippa Bell

Levels	*Any*
Aims	*Become aware of the many helpful similarities between English words and words in the first language*
Class Time	*10 minutes*
Preparation Time	*5 minutes*
Resources	*Level-appropriate reading passage, ideally with line numbers*

PROCEDURE

1. Chose a prominent cognate word from the beginning of the reading passage. For example, if learners are Spanish speakers and they will read the fable of the frog and the scorpion, the word *scorpion* is a good choice (*escorpión*).

2. Ask students what they think the word means and to provide the translation equivalent. Point out that this is an example of a "good friend" and explain the term *cognate* if students are not familiar with it already.

3. Ask students to look at the passage and circle all the cognates they can find in it. This can be done individually or in pairs. Since cognates do not always match exactly in terms of their spellings (e.g., *scorpion/escorpión*), encourage students to also look for words that they think may be cognates.

4. Finding cognates can be done as a race. When the time is up, students count up the number of words they have highlighted. The winners are those who find the most.

5. As you go over the findings with students, ask them to provide the first language equivalents and to circle any that they may have missed.

6. Finally, ask students if they were surprised to find so many. Guide the discussion toward the conclusion that one's first language can be very helpful in understanding new English words.

CAVEATS AND OPTIONS

1. This activity works well as a re-reading exercise once students have already worked with the passage in some other way. It is also a useful prereading activity.

2. The aim is to highlight the availability of good friends, but be prepared to explain any false friends that may be found.

3. Keep an eye out for cognate patterns, and group any words that fit a particular pattern together on the board. Then ask students to try to come up with a rule. For example, if the learners are Spanish speakers, ask what they notice about *scorpion, school,* and *space* and the way they correspond to the Spanish equivalents *escorpión, escuela,* and *espacio.* (Answer: initial *es* in Spanish = *s* only in English.) Highlighting patterns is important because students may not notice them on their own.

4. The number of cognates found will vary depending on the students' first language. In the case of European languages, there are many—often many more than students expect.

5. The learners' first language may not lend itself to this activity. Friendly English cognates are less available to speakers of more "distant" languages.

REFERENCES AND FURTHER READING

Horst, M., White, J., & Bell, P. (2010). First and second language knowledge in the language classroom. *International Journal of Bilingualism, 14,* 331–349. doi:10.1177/1367006910367848

Moss, G. (1992). Cognate recognition: Its importance in the teaching of ESP reading courses to Spanish speakers. *English for Specific Purposes, 11*(2), 141–158. doi:10.1016/S0889-4906(05)80005-5

White, J., & Horst, M. (2012). Cognate awareness-raising in late childhood: Teachable and useful. *Language Awareness, 21,* 181–196.

IV

Homophone Business

Solihin Agyl

Levels	*Pre-intermediate to high intermediate*
Aims	*Improve autonomous learning through vocabulary building*
Class Time	*30 minutes*
Preparation Time	*None*
Resources	*100 homophones on cards*
	Five slips of paper with $2 written on each of them for each student in the class

PROCEDURE

1. Give students access to English-English learner's dictionaries containing phonetic symbols.

2. Make sure all students understand what a homophone is because they will deal with pair words with exactly the same pronunciation but different spellings.

3. Distribute the homophones in the Appendix to students equally so that each student gets five to use as goods in this activity. Check that students recognize and know the meanings of their homophones. Homophone lists can be found online at www.homophone.com.

4. Hand out five of the money-like slips of paper for students to use for the buying and selling activity; each student should have $10 as their capital in the business.

5. Tell students that they are going to be businesspeople who want to sell all their homophones (goods) and get money. Each homophone costs $2. However, when a homophone is going to be sold to you, the seller is obliged to tell you the other word with the same pronunciation.

6. Students can also sell homophones to another student at their own price (more than the $2 minimum).

7. Participants may get bonus words—with prices that you set—provided among the homophones. However, not every single homophone will

be endorsed as a bonus word. The idea with bonus words is to increase students' ambition to sell and buy any word they think they can work on, thereby eventually getting the most money and winning the game. The winner of this business activity is the one with the most money and with no more homophones left in the hand.

8. The activity works best when all participants mingle freely to buy and sell, to check one another's homophones, to communicate and lobby, to offer, to persuade and influence, and even to consult in order to eventually accomplish their mission of winning the game.

CAVEATS AND OPTIONS

1. For lower-level students, some frequently used classroom language can be introduced in this activity. For example, "How do you pronounce it/this/that word?," "How do you spell it/this/that?," "How do you pronounce ____ in English?," "How do you spell ____ in English?" (Students may even come up with the first language word.)

2. Some daily business terminology is also needed. For example, "I'd like to sell this word," "Would you like to sell it/this/that word?," "Can I buy it/this/that word?," "Would you like to buy it/this/that word?," "How much is it/this/that?"

3. Easier homophones should be used for lower level students. "*Horse/Hoarse*," for instance, is not suggested for students of lower level.

4. This activity can be changed into a spelling activity mingled with word-by-word translation like a spelling bee for lower levels. This way, students, especially children, will become more emotionally involved in the lesson, as I frequently see in my elementary classes.

5. This vocabulary build-up technique can also be applied using collocations, phrasal verbs, compound nouns, and idioms instead of homophones.

IV

REFERENCES AND FURTHER READING

Oxford, R. L. (1990). *Language learning strategies: What every teacher should know.* Boston, MA: Heinle & Heinle.

APPENDIX: *Homophones to Distribute to Learners*

allowed	blue	berry	cereal	days
road	higher	key	nose	male
horse	principle	pier	miner	gilt
saw	through	way	wear	board
which	cue	die	guest	least
morning	praise	stare	tax	whether
bowled	sealing	frays	hole	heard
tea	pair	paste	rain	sent
bear	heal	fair	feet	hall

A Zammechat Lesson in Vocabulary

Alex Dawson

Levels	*Intermediate +*
Aims	*Understand unknown words from context*
Class Time	*30–45 minutes*
Preparation time	*5 minutes*
Resources	*Unknown words handout (see Appendix)*

PROCEDURE

1. Introduce the concept of understanding unknown words in context. Here are some suggested strategies:

   - Look at the target words in the text. What word form is the unknown word in the text? Is it a noun, verb, adjective, adverb? Look at the position of the word in the sentence, the surrounding words (e.g., *the* and *a* are normally followed by a noun or adjective), and the construction of the word (e.g., the suffix *–ment* is added to nouns, the prefix *un–* suggests negativity).

   - Look at the surrounding context of the word. What is the relationship between the unknown word and other phrases? For example, in the sentence *The man put the XXX on his head to keep warm and then walked away*, we know that *XXX* refers to an object (noun), it is small and light enough to put on his head and walk away, and the purpose of putting it on his head was to keep warm, therefore it is probably a hat.

2. Put this example sentence on the board, and ask learners to try to guess the meaning of the words in **bold** using the two strategies above.

   > So thinking like this with my gulliver bent and my rookers stuck in my trouser carmans I walked the town.

   Here is a possible solution:

   a. **gulliver:** (1) singular noun, (2) belonging to the writer (from "my"). What "bends" while walking: *a person's back or neck perhaps?*

IV

b. **carmans:** (1) plural noun, (2) connected to trousers and the writer puts his "rookers" in them: *pockets perhaps?*

c. **rookers:** (1) plural noun, (2) belonging to the writer, and are in trouser "carmens"/pockets: *hands perhaps?*

3. Discuss which strategies students used for guessing the meanings of the unknown words in the example.

4. Next, get learners to look at a longer piece of text and practise their guessing strategies. Below is a sample text from *A Clockwork Orange,* by Anthony Burgess, in which characters speak in a strange version of English that uses many imaginary words. Students could work in pairs using this text.

> I walked the town, and at last I began to feel very tired and also in great need of a nice **bolshy chasha** of milky **chai**. Thinking about this **chai**, I got a sudden like picture of me sitting before a **bolshy** fire in an armchair **peeting** away at this **chai**, and what was funny and very very strange was that I seemed to have turned into a very starry **chelloveck**, about seventy years old, because I could **viddy** my own **voloss**, which was very grey, and I also had whiskers, and these were very grey too. I came to one of these tea-and-coffee **mestos**, and I could **viddy** through the long long window that it was full of very dull **lewdies**, like ordinary, who had these very patient and expressionless **litsos** and would do no harm to no one, all sitting there and **govoreeting** like quietly and **peeting** away at their nice harmless **chai** and coffee. I **ittied** inside and went up to the counter and bought a nice hot **chai** with plenty of **moloko.** (Burgess, 1962, p. 148)

CAVEATS AND OPTIONS

1. Divide the class into two teams, A and B. Each team will invent a story using a mixture of other unknown or difficult words from *A Clockwork Orange* (see the Appendix). The story can be anything they choose, perhaps about meeting friends in town, a strange journey, or an incident while shopping. The purpose of this activity is to help learners use the strategy of guessing meaning from context in listening. Students should show their stories to someone from the other team.

2. Because these words are actually not real, you could substitute real but obscure words taken from the dictionary that students are unlikely to know.

REFERENCES AND FURTHER READING

Burgess, A. (1962). *A clockwork orange.* London, England: Heinemann.

APPENDIX: *Unknown or Difficult Words From* A Clockwork Orange

Team A

Word	English "Translation"
cantor	office
brosay	to throw
cheena	woman
gooly	to walk
dobby	good
ookadeet	to leave
veshch	thing
polezny	useful
sabog	shoe
molodoy	young

Team B

Word	English "Translation"
collocoll	bell
crast	to steal
choondessny	wonderful
gromky	loud
grahzny	dirty
pony	to understand
privodeet	to lead somewhere
slovo	word
shlem	helmet
tomtick	piece

IV

Brain-Power Vocabulary Techniques

Guowu Jiang

Levels	*All*
Aims	*Develop vocabulary knowledge from morpheme to context levels*
	Use visualisation to facilitate memorization
Class Time	*45 minutes*
Preparation Time	*20 minutes*
Resources	*5–10 target words*

PROCEDURE

1. Select 5–10 target words that learners need to learn, and provide the central and basic meanings of the words in both English and the first language translation.

2. Explain to students that they will be using the same target words to work through a series of activities that are associated with developing "brain power" techniques.

3. The first activity is application. Give each student one copy of Figure 1, the Application Framework, which involves the aspects of vocabulary knowledge from the word to context levels.

4. Choose a target word to work with in class. For example, if you choose the word *academic*, students can work with you to produce the following information in either written or spoken format:

   - word parts: *academ*[*y*] + *ic*

   - individual words: *academic, educational, scholarly,* etc.

   - family words: *academy, academia, academically*

   - words in phrases: *academic vocabulary, academic integrity*

   - words in sentences: *the university has an outstanding academic reputation*

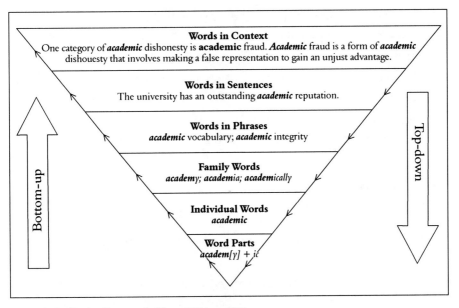

Figure 1. *Application Framework (Jiang, 2014, p. 122)*

- words in context: *one category of academic dishonesty is academic fraud; academic fraud is a form of academic dishonesty that involves making a false representation to gain an unjust advantage*

5. Have students work in pairs or groups to work on their own target words using the Application Framework.

6. The second activity is visualisation. Give students a piece of blank paper each, and ask them to draw the exact image which the target words convey in their mind, from word to context levels. For example, with the word *apple*, ask students to draw pictures to illustrate the target word used in different levels, as in the following:

An apple   An apple tree   A bear in front of a big apple tree with many apples

(Images from Royalty-free Microstock Image Library.)

7. Then ask students to visualise in their mind the meanings projected by the target words, phrases, and sentences. Have them draw images to illustrate the words.

8. Ask students to stand up and share their own pictures to illustrate the words, phrases, and sentences with their peers and read them aloud.

9. Discuss the two activities presented here as a class and how learners might use these techniques for their vocabulary learning in future.

CAVEATS AND OPTIONS

1. Information on word parts is available at http://wordinfo.info.

2. Skip the word parts step if some words cannot be further deconstructed into morphemes.

3. The six levels of vocabulary knowledge can be used either selectively or individually based on learning needs. For example, you can have students deal with the target words in the collocation and syntactic levels only.

4. Learners might need several attempts at this activity to fully understand all levels of the pyramid.

REFERENCES AND FURTHER READING

Jiang, G. (2014). *EFL/ESL vocabulary teaching strategies: The effects of bottom-up and top-down approaches on the acquisition of EFL/ESL vocabulary by Chinese university students* (Unpublished doctoral dissertation). University of Newcastle, Australia.

Sousa, D. (2001). *How the brain learns* (2nd ed.). Thousand Oaks, CA: Corwin.

Learners Teach "Found Outside the Classroom" Vocabulary

Julie Bytheway

Levels	*Multilevel*
Aims	*Raise awareness of autonomous vocabulary learning outside the classroom*
Class Time	*Less than 5 minutes per learner per repetition*
Preparation Time	*None*

Learners usually know their peers. Encourage learners to share good places to autonomously learn vocabulary, and trust learners to help others remember (not forget) the vocabulary they teach. This task also provides learners with an opportunity for meaning-focused speaking (output) and learning through teaching.

PROCEDURE

1. Ask learners to make a schedule so that at the beginning of each lesson one or two learners teach two words to the class.

2. When it is a learner's turn, he or she finds two interesting words from life outside the classroom and teaches these two words to the class.

3. Learners must justify why the words are useful (e.g., *fatal* means causing death or the end or a disaster or failure and can be used in health contexts but also regarding ideas and plans and actions).

4. They must show examples of use of the word (e.g., A heart attack can be fatal, Any mistake could be fatal and our team could lose the challenge).

5. They must say specifically where they found the words (e.g., a TV programme).

6. They must help the class remember the words (e.g., *fatal* is like *fate tell* and fate always tells bad news).

IV

CAVEATS AND OPTIONS

1. When increasing learners' responsibility for learning and teaching, you may need to explain and justify the value of the learning tasks to learners, parents, colleagues, and administrators.

2. Learners can use any resources to help teach the word that they think is helpful (e.g., messaged to a Facebook group to see on their mobile devices, Prezi presentation on a SMART Board, written on paper handouts).

3. High school students who are infrequently (high stakes) assessed from speeches in front of the whole class can use this activity as a (low stakes) opportunity to speak in front of the whole class.

4. Learners can teach their words to the whole class or a small group.

5. You can make a vocabulary test from words students' select and teach, and learners can get feedback about how effective their vocabulary teaching was from an (anonymous) overview of the class test results.

Rank and Adapt Vocabulary Learning Strategies Used Outside Classrooms

Julie Bytheway

Levels	*Intermediate to advanced*
Aims	*Raise awareness of vocabulary learning strategies*
Class Time	*10–20 minutes*
Preparation Time	*None*

PROCEDURE

1. In small discussion groups, ask learners to brainstorm at least five specific ways they autonomously learn vocabulary outside the classroom (e.g., YouTube videos, digital games, conversations with speakers of the target language). Have learners record their brainstorm in writing.

2. After a set time, or when learners appear to be nearly finished, ask them to rank their vocabulary learning strategies in order of learning effectiveness. Which ones make learning easier or more lasting or more meaningful? Learners may need to be reminded to consider a wide variety of factors, including social and emotional needs as well as cognitive and metacognitive learning needs. Learners negotiate their ranking and then record their ranking order in writing.

3. Again after a set time, or when learners appear to be nearly finished, ask them to describe specific ways that their two most effective vocabulary learning strategies can be used inside classrooms. How can in-classroom learning be adapted so that these two vocabulary learning strategies can be used effectively?

CAVEATS AND OPTIONS

1. This activity may work better when learners have previously been made aware of examples of vocabulary strategies used inside the classroom.

IV

2. Small groups and individual learners may need guidance, through a series of probing questions, before they are able to describe the vocabulary learning strategies they use outside the classroom.

3. When increasing learners' responsibility for learning and teaching, you may need to explain and justify the value of the learning tasks to learners, parents, colleagues, and administrators.

4. Learners can then trial and reflect on effectiveness of transfer of vocabulary strategies from outside classroom contexts to inside classroom contexts, and then learners can further adapt strategies to improve their own learning.

5. Learners can also describe specific ways vocabulary learning strategies used in one context outside the classroom can be adapted for a different context outside the classroom.

6. Learners can be invited as guests in other classes to teach other learners how to create, select, use, and transfer vocabulary learning strategies.

7. Learners can create an online wiki to share trial of, reflection on, and further adaption of vocabulary learning strategies with other learners and teachers.

8. Learners can teach teachers how to teach vocabulary learning strategies to other learners and other teachers.

REFERENCES AND FURTHER READING

Nation, P. (2008). *Teaching vocabulary: Strategies and techniques*. Boston, MA: Heinle/Cengage Learning.

Nation, P., & Gu, P. Y. (2007). *Focus on vocabulary*. Sydney, Australia: Macquarie University, National Centre for English Language Teaching and Research.

Haptic-Assisted Vocabulary and Pronunciation Teaching Technique

Michael Burri

Levels	*Upper beginner, middle school age +*
Aims	*Learn, pronounce, and practice new vocabulary containing lax vowels*
Class Time	*2–3 minutes per word*
Preparation Time	*30 minutes*
Resources	*10 words containing lax vowels*
	Vowel Clock (see Appendix)
	Haptic video for introduction: https://vimeo.com/60977241

aptic refers to a systematic combination of movement and touch used by instructors to teach pronunciation to second language learners. In the haptic system (henceforth AH-EPS, for Acton Haptic English Pronunciation System) lax vowels are called rough vowels. The learning of new words containing lax vowels in AH-EPS involves five steps that encompass movement, touch, corresponding numbers, key words, and vowel sounds. Each of the five steps is briefly outlined below, using the word *interesting* as an example. The aim is to introduce this technique to learners and encourage them to use it in their independent vocabulary learning.

IV

PROCEDURE

1. Identify the number of syllables in a word, for example, four syllables in *interesting*: in ▪ ter ▪ est ▪ ing (tap thumb and middle finger together on each syllable).

2. Identify the stressed syllable in a word, for example, **in** ▪ ter ▪ est ▪ ing (use same procedure as in Step 1, but open hand rapidly on stressed syllable).

3. Identify the vowel in the stressed syllable, for example, **in** ▪ ter ▪ est ▪ ing (vowel #2; see Vowel Clock).

4. Say the word aloud and with enthusiasm, while at the same time touching the right palm with the tip of the middle finger of the left hand on the stressed syllable **in** at about 2 o'clock in the visual field. Do that three times. This process helps learners memorize the new word.

5. Say a sentence containing the new word as you again touch the right palm with the tip of the middle finger of the left hand on the stressed syllable **in**, for example, "this class is **in**teresting." Do that three times. The purpose is to anchor the word in learners' memories by engaging multiple modalities (sight, movement, touch, hearing, speaking) at the same time.

CAVEATS AND OPTIONS

1. The haptic component can also be used to provide students with timely corrective feedback on their pronunciation of words. For example, if a student says *pit* instead of *pet*, you can demonstrate *pit* (vowel #2) and then *pet* (vowel #4) to establish a visual picture of the different vowel positioning on the clock (for a more detailed account, see Acton, Baker, Burri, Teaman, 2013).

2. You and students can also practice one vowel at a time and learn the haptic movements together. For example, you and students can practice a list of words containing the same vowel sound until both parties feel comfortable expressing it haptically. This process helps both you and them gain confidence before moving on to learn other sounds and movements.

3. Word lists can be assigned as homework, based on the same five-step procedure outlined above.

4. The IPA symbols used in the Vowel Clock may change based on dialect, particularly in the lower half of the clock.

REFERENCES AND FURTHER READING

Acton, W. (2013). *Haptic-integrated clinical pronunciation research.* Retrieved from http://hipoeces.blogspot.com.au

Actonhaptic.com features several additional haptic videos. The videos are available at http://www.actonhaptic.com/#!demos/c1yws

Acton, W., Baker, A., Burri, M., & Teaman, B. (2013). Preliminaries to haptic-integrated pronunciation instruction. In J. M. Levis & K. LeVelle (Eds.), *Proceedings of the 4th Pronunciation in Second Language Learning and Teaching Conference* (pp. 234–244). Ames: Iowa State University.

Teaman, B., & Acton, W. (2013). Haptic (movement and touch for better) pronunciation. In N. Sonda & A. Krause (Eds.), *JALT 2012 Conference Proceedings* (pp. 402–409). Tokyo, Japan: JALT. Retrieved from http://jalt-publications.org/proceedings/articles/3285-haptic-movement-and-touch-better-pronunciation

APPENDIX: *Vowel Clock*

For students to practice and learn vocabulary systematically and efficiently, the lax vowels in AH-EPS are aligned with numbers on a clock.

Designed by Karen Rauser (used with permission) and based on AH-EPS.

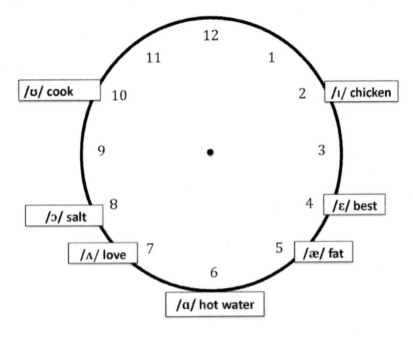

Vocabulary and Technology

- **Finding Out More About Words**
- **Words and Phrases in Context**
- **Revising Vocabulary Using Technology**

V

Part V: Vocabulary and Technology

Technology is a rapidly changing area in vocabulary teaching as more and more websites and tools become available to support vocabulary planning, teaching, and learning. In some countries, tablets are becoming the main interface for learning tools, rather than pen and paper, which is why there is a range of activities here based on particular applications or apps that can be downloaded for mobile phones, tablets, or laptops and used by teachers and learners. Other activities are based on free websites or tools that teachers and learners can use. There can be no doubt that examples of language in use (single words and multiword units) are in abundance online and in apps and are readily accessible for learners and teachers.

One of the key points about technology in vocabulary is the high level of motivation and interest that they can encourage in learners and the large amount of words and phrases that are presented in context to learners. Coxhead and Bytheway (in press) look at two very popular online activities for language learners, TED Talks and massively multiplayer online role-playing games (MMORPGs). They found that these online environments include a great deal of input, many opportunities for repetition of lexical items, and multiple chances for learners to notice language in use. MMORPGs in particular also provide high levels of meaningful interaction with other players online. Opportunities for output and language practice are important, as we know, and online environments are more and more able to deliver that kind of practice to learners.

The four strands (Nation, 2007) can apply to online vocabulary learning opportunities as they can to paper-based or more traditional activities. Technology has also influenced vocabulary learning techniques for learners because they can amass their own examples of language in use for analysis using corpora or using the Internet as a corpus. See Charles (2012) for a full discussion of learners using corpus techniques to learn collocations and Cobb (n.d.) and this section of this book for a range of vocabulary-focused activities in English and several other languages using corpora. Technology can also be used to find out more about words through activities that focus on aspects of words such as spelling, pronunciation, common collocations, and phrases.

Note that by this stage in the book, common threads come through from other parts of the book, such as multiword units (for example, see "Concordance Search," by Tom Cobb in this part of the book) and developing autonomy using websites and online tools for study outside class (and inside, too). Plenty of revision activities for vocabulary can be found online also. Some of these activities

V

can look quite similar to their paper-based predecessors, whereas others have moved away from the more traditional formats. Principles such as regular and often practice can be easily applied in these online environments, but there is still the challenge of having learners then apply what they have practiced to their speaking and writing offline.

REFERENCES AND FURTHER READING

Charles, M. (2012). "Proper vocabulary and juicy collocations": EAP students evaluate do-it-yourself corpus-building. *English for Specific Purposes, 31*, 93–102. doi:10.1016/j.esp.2011.12.003

Cobb, T. (n.d.). *The compleat lexical tutor.* Retrieved from http://www.lextutor.ca

Coxhead, A., & Bytheway, J. (in press). Learning vocabulary using two massive online resources: You will not blink. In D. Nunan & J. Richards (Eds.), *Learning beyond the classroom.* Oxford, England: Routledge.

Nation, I. S. P. (2007). The four strands. *Innovation in language learning and teaching, 1*(1), 2–13. doi:10.2167/illt039.0

Words in Word

Feifei Han

Levels	*Beginner to intermediate*
Aims	*Learn new words in Microsoft Word*
	Learn new words in daily life
Class Time	*10–15 minutes*
Preparation Time	*5 minutes*
Resources	*Computers or laptops with Microsoft Word installed*
	Dictionaries (students bring their own, or prepare some for them)

ost students know how to use word-processing software, but they may ignore that these programs can also serve as good resources for learning new English vocabulary. This activity demonstrates how words can be learnt through using technology. It also opens up new channels for students to explore new words in their daily life.

PROCEDURE

1. Ask students to brainstorm in small groups the words they already know related to Microsoft Word as a warm-up activity. Some examples of words might be *file*, *delete*, and *save a document*. Have them check in groups that they all know the meanings of the words they have brainstormed.

2. Ask students to open a Microsoft Word document and work in groups, in pairs, or individually to find out five new words in Word Tools located at the top of the Word document. Some possible new words could be *layout*, *references*, *format*, *clipboard*, *paste*, *heading*, *select*, *replace*, *edit*, *font*, and *paragraph*.

3. For each new word, ask students to guess its meaning first according to its function in Word and to write down their inference in the worksheet provided (see Appendix).

4. Then ask them to look up the meaning of these words in a dictionary, to confirm or disconfirm their inference, and to write down the meaning of the word in the worksheet.

5. Have them exchange words they have found with another student in the class.

CAVEATS AND OPTIONS

1. You can decide how many new words you would like students to find depending on time available for this activity.

2. If there is only one computer available, you can show the whole class how they can learn some new words using Word.

3. You can tell students that learning new words can also be achieved by using Microsoft Excel, Microsoft PowerPoint, Adobe, and other similar software. You should also raise learners' awareness of how words can be learnt and accumulated in daily activities.

4. You may introduce students to this activity briefly without asking them to do it in classes. You can ask students to learn new words and keep a learning journal themselves as a kind of after-class activity. Students may hand in their learning journals at the end of a certain period (e.g., 1 month, 3 months, one semester).

APPENDIX: *Sample Worksheet*

New Words	Your Inference	Correct (✓) or Incorrect (x) Inference	Meaning
e.g., *insert*	to put sth into sth	✓	to put or set into, between, or among

Spelling Activities With Educreations Interactive Whiteboard

Helen Bowen

Levels	*Lower*
Aims	*Learn the correspondence between the grapheme and sound of the short vowel a*
Class Time	*1.5–2 hours*
Preparation Time	*30 minutes*
Resources	*iPad with Educreations app*

This activity is especially useful for motivating and engaging students who have difficulties with English spelling, especially with short vowels (e.g., native Arabic speakers).

PROCEDURE

1. Prepare a list of single-syllable words containing *a* (for practice in isolation), such as *man, pan, hand, cat,* and *sat.* These are easy to find, but you can also look in any basic phonics book.

2. Prepare a list of minimal pairs for discrimination practice, such as *man/men, sat/sit, pan/pen.*

3. Prepare a list or words with one or two syllables containing *a* (not schwa), such as *apple, handsome,* and *sandwich.* Use common words that students know and/or have problems with.

4. Clearly model the sound /a/ and show the written letter. Have students practice the /a/ sound. Do not let students use the name of the letter, only the sound.

5. Drill the *a* words in isolation, with students reading and repeating at the same time, first altogether, then individually.

6. Repeat the procedure with the discrimination exercise. Students can work in pairs to see if their partner can identify which word they chose. Students can also do mutual dictations.

7. Students identify the *a* vowel in multisyllable words and say them.

8. Connect your iPad to a projector (if you have one) to demonstrate for the class how to use Educreations. Show students how to

   • take and insert new photos from the camera roll or web,

   •. use the keyboard or pen to add text,

   •. record themselves.

9. Give students a list of *a* words.

10. For each word, students insert a picture, copy the word, and record themselves (see the Appendix for examples).

11. Students can email their exercise to you as a movie (to include the recording), or they can save it to a personal folder or portfolio. They can also project their work in class or make posters for the classroom.

CAVEATS AND OPTIONS

1. For students to truly focus on the vowel in single-syllable and multisyllable words, it's important that you use known lexis in this activity. If you use first language phonics books as a source of words, be careful to select items which are known to learners.

2. This lesson can be replicated with other short vowels and problem sounds (e.g., *b/p*). It's also useful to show how adding the silent *e* and other suffixes (e.g., *–ing, –ed, –er*) changes the pronunciation and spelling of words. This activity can be used for spelling practice in class, for homework, or for assessment purposes.

3. Other easy apps which can be used are Explain Everything (paid) or any app with the facility to draw/import pictures, use a pen or keyboard, and record.

4. One word of caution is that apps are constantly changing, so look at what is available and choose the best one at the time.

APPENDIX: *Student Examples*

Examples of students' hand-drawn pictures and handwritten words with short *a* (recorded)	Examples of personal photographs with typed words with short *e* (recorded)

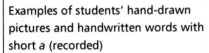

V

Explain Everything to Help Poor Spellers

Helen Bowen

Levels	Lower
Aims	Break down multisyllable words into syllables
	Understand that each syllable has one vowel sound
Class Time	45–60 minutes
Preparation Time	15 minutes
Resources	iPad with Explain Everything app

This activity is helpful for any students who have difficulties with English spelling, especially where they appear to rely on visual memory without auditory strategies like sounding out words. It helps engage and motivate students in learning to break down multisyllable words into syllables, which are easier to spell. Students learn that each syllable has one vowel sound (including *y*), so every vowel sound equals one syllable (e.g., ch**ee**se vs. ch**ee**s-**y).

PROCEDURE

1. Prepare a table with four columns, labelled 1 syllable, 2 syllables, and so on, as shown in Appendix A. The table can be saved as a picture on a shared site so students can import it as a picture into the apps, or it can be given to students on paper, which they can photograph after they have written in the words.

2. Prepare a list of about 20–24 words of course vocabulary, common words you want students to know, or words they have problems spelling or saying (e.g., *clothes*). Make sure there is a mix of word lengths. Add words to the bottom of the table, as shown in Appendix A.

3. Clearly model how to sound out a one-syllable word (e.g., *pen*). Make sure to use your hand to show the beat. Repeat with similar words. Students practise with you.

4. Repeat with two-syllable words (e.g., *pencil, paper*).

5. Connect your iPad to a projector (if you have one), to demonstrate how to use Explain Everything to the class. Show students how to

   - access the table from where you have saved it and insert it as a photo into the app,

   - use the keyboard or pen to write words in the correct column. (Click on the pen and hold down the icon for options or A for text and double-click on the screen for the keyboard.)

6. Students sound out words and write them in the correct column (see Appendix B). Monitor the class, making sure that students are beating out the syllables with their hands.

7. Check the answers.

8. Show students how to record themselves with the red button (bottom of screen).

9. Get students to carefully record themselves reading each list, making sure to sound out only the appropriate number of syllables.

10. Students can email their exercise to you as a movie (to include the recording), or they can save it to a personal folder or portfolio. Use export buttons.

CAVEATS AND OPTIONS

1. As with any teaching, it's important to focus on the main aim of the activity. The focus of the lesson outlined here is pronunciation and spelling. Therefore, make sure that the words you use in the table are words which students know. You don't want to get distracted by explaining the meaning of vocabulary items, thus lessening students' attention to the syllables and vowels within them.

2. There can be some confusion about the number of syllables in some words, depending on pronunciation. For example, some people say *fam-ly*, but try to reinforce the "one vowel sound equals one syllable" rule and stress *fam-i-ly*.

3. You may prefer to give students a paper worksheet on which to handwrite the words. In this case, ask students to take a photo of their worksheet with their iPad and import the picture from the camera roll into the chosen app.

4. This activity can also be done using similar apps, such as Educreations or any other app with a facility to draw/import pictures, add text, and record.

V

APPENDIX A: *Student Worksheet*

Sounding Out Syllables to Help With Spelling

1 syllable	2 syllables	3 syllables	4 syllables
book	student	Arabic	Emirati

Say these words and then write them in the correct column above:

pen	pencil	family	reads	woman	computer
clothes	learn	binder	file	centre	banana
television	homework	want	study	children	am
Internet	listening	timetable	paper	company	married

APPENDIX B: *Example of a Student's Completed Worksheet*

1 syllable	2 syllables	3 syllables	4 syllables
book	student	Arabic	Emirati
pen	pencil	computer	television
reads	woman	banana	
learn	binder	Internet	
file	centre	family	
want	homework	listening	
clothes	study	timetable	
am	children	company	
	paper		
	married		

Concordance Search

Marlise Horst, Tom Cobb, and Ioana Nicolae

Levels	*Intermediate +*
Aims	*Gain deep knowledge of new words, including collocation, grammatical use, register, and multiple senses*
	Become aware of different aspects of word knowledge
	Get familiar with computer tools for discovery learning
Class Time	*30 minutes*
Preparation Time	*20 minutes*
Resources	*Computers with Internet access*
	Worksheet or projection (Appendix A)

PROCEDURE

1. Select three or four words from a class reading or activity that you judge are important for students to know in more depth. An example might be *contract*, which comes from Coxhead's (2000) Academic Word List, a list of words that are important for university-bound learners to know.

2. Start investigating the word by clicking on the "Concordance" link at the Compleat Lexical Tutor website (www.lextutor.ca). Then select "Corpus-based concordances: English."

3. Type *contract* (or one of the words you have selected) into the keyword box. Change the default "exact" option to the "family" option.

4. Select a suitable corpus. For example, if students are high-intermediate university-bound learners, and the investigated word is *contract*, the University Word List corpus is a good choice. For less advanced learners and more basic words, the 1k or 2k Graded Readers corpus may be more suitable, and advanced learners can work with the much larger and more comprehensive BNC corpora.

5. Once a corpus has been selected, click on "Get concordance." In the example of *contract* and the University Word List corpus, 98 lines will appear (15 lines are shown in Appendix B to illustrate).

V

6. Since students may be unsure of what to look for in this output, devise questions that show them where to look. It can take the form of a worksheet with questions for each of the words you have opted to work with. Ideally, the questions focus first on simple, easy-to-see discoveries and then move to more challenging aspects. A good starting point is the different forms of the word—an aspect that is easy to assess by looking at the highlighted words in the center of the output page. Thus in the case of *contract*, additional forms such as *contracts, contracted,* and *contractor* can be found.

7. See Appendix A for a sequence of questions that progress from simple to more complex tasks.

CAVEATS AND OPTIONS

1. A resource for selecting words that are important for learners of English to know is the "Famous frequency lists" link on the Compleat Lexical Tutor site (click the "Frequency" link on the homepage).

2. Before students start investigating the selected words in the computer lab, verify that all of them actually occur in the corpus you have chosen and that there are enough output lines for students to make useful generalizations. This is important!

3. It is useful to demonstrate the tools by working on the first few words together. Students need to become familiar with the concordance format.

4. Students can click on the target word in a concordance line to see the complete sentence context. There is also a link to an online dictionary at the top of the output.

REFERENCES AND FURTHER READING

Cobb, T. (1997). Is there any measurable learning from hands-on concordancing? *System, 25*, 301–315.

Cobb, T. (1999). Breadth and depth of vocabulary acquisition with hands-on concordancing. *Computer Assisted Language Learning, 12*, 345–360.

Coxhead, A. (2000). A new academic word list. *TESOL Quarterly, 34*, 213–238.

Horst, M., Cobb, T., & Nicolae, I. (2005). Expanding academic vocabulary with an online collaborative word bank. *Language Learning and Technology, 9*, 90–110.

APPENDIX A: *Concordance Questions*

1. What other forms of the word do you see in the concordance lines? Which one occurs most often?

2. What do you notice about the grammar of the word? Is it a noun, verb, adjective, or adverb?

3. Find one line that you can easily understand. Ignore any lines that are unclear. Is the meaning of the word in this line the same as the meaning used in class?

4. Find several more lines that you can easily understand. What does this word usually mean? Is there more than one meaning?

5. What kinds of topics use this word? Is it a scientific word? A business word? Something else?

6. Now scroll to the bottom of the output. What word is most often used to the immediate left of the word? (This is the left collocate.)

7. Return to the input page and change the setting under "Controls" to "Sort by one to the right." What word is most often used to the immediate right (the right collocate)?

8. Write a sentence about ____ (specify a topic) using the word and its most often used right collocate.

9. Did anything about your investigation of this word surprise you? Explain.

APPENDIX B: *Sample From University Word List Corpus*

Concordance for *family* **CONTRACT**

1. "to work? Twenty years ago, there was such a thing as a "<u>contract</u> worker"? The worker world isn't what it used to be

2. the growth and development of the business sector. "<u>Contracts</u> of employment are agreements between employees and employers.

3. nodded sagely and pulled out a "found property" form. THE "<u>contract</u> between the generations" that underlies most

4. hares were the most actively traded option. More than 2,000 <u>contracts</u> were completed. Standard Chartered, the banking

5. was also the busiest option stock, claiming nearly 2,800 <u>contracts</u>. It was suggested that Goldsmith interests already had

V

6. following extensive option trading with more than 3,200 <u>contracts</u>, was at one time down 5.5 p at 57 p. The shares . . .

7. to owners of McDonald's fanchisees. They will enter into a <u>contract</u> with patent holders to handle "product," the . . .

8. awareness clauses or mandatory anything. They just work. A <u>contract</u> employee can charge double the cost of a regular . . .

9. government might otherwise have raised. "Clearly, when a <u>contract</u> is breached, it is wise to consider first any need . . .

10. resident of the National League. Shell has yet to discuss a <u>contract</u> with Davis, but said: I have no problem with that.

11. six hundred foreign workers on standby ready to work on a <u>contract</u> basis. In knowledge industries, brainpower is the . . .

12. to the board, "when the government with full knowledge of a <u>contractor's</u> quality-control procedure permits the . . .

13. more than 67m over the next four years, an extension of a <u>contract</u> in which it is paid £10.5m over five years. The debt . . .

14. Bonn to determine whether the proposed sale will go ahead. <u>Contract</u> discussions have been underway since early this year . . .

15. Overseas—except for South Africa—during the winter. Any <u>contracted</u> player under the age of 22 will be eligible.

Mobile Vocabulary Learning Through Photo Blogging

Michael Madson

Levels	**Any**
Aims	**Acquire vocabulary through associations with blog photos and descriptions**
Class Time	**15–25 minutes**
Preparation Time	**20–30 minutes**
Resources	**Smartphones**
	An account with a blogging platform, such as Blogger or WordPress

PROCEDURE

1. Compile a list of vocabulary for students to learn. The list may relate to the course textbook (if any), a language task, or their personal interests and goals. How much vocabulary to assign depends on students' language proficiency. At beginning levels, one vocabulary word per student should be doable. (Thus, you would compile 20 vocabulary words for a class of 20 students, for example.) At more advanced levels, consider challenging the class with two or three vocabulary words per student.

2. Create an account with a blogging platform, and send invitations for students to join as contributors.

3. Divide the class into pairs, and assign vocabulary to each pair. The number of vocabulary words, again, will vary with students' proficiency levels. Explain that their task is to take and upload a photo for each vocabulary word assigned to them. Each photo should be accompanied by a one-paragraph explanation, helping blog readers understand the connection between the word's meanings and the uploaded photo. Sample sentences that use the assigned vocabulary are also appropriate.

4. Read the blog posts, and check that students have understood the meanings of the vocabulary assigned to them. Consider offering feedback in the comments, such as grammar corrections (e.g., "Do you mean 'The executive

V

offered to *make* a deal?'") or responses to content itself (e.g., "Hmm, I don't quite see the photo's connection to the vocabulary here. Please revise.").

The commenting function is already built in to the blogging platform. As long as commenting is enabled, all you need to do is type and post.

5. If time permits, invite the pairs to share their blog entries (the vocabulary words, photos, and paragraphs) in class.

6. Quiz students on the entire vocabulary list. If much of the class struggled with a particular word, ask the pair assigned to that word to upload another photo and paragraph.

7. When the class is ready, divide it into new pairs, and repeat the activity. Continue to refer to the photo blog throughout the course, and encourage—or require—students to use the words they learn in their speaking and writing. Depending on its effectiveness and on students' interest, this activity might be used two or three times per term.

CAVEATS AND OPTIONS

1. Make sure to first familiarize yourself with the blogging platform you intend to use. Otherwise, carrying out this activity—and responding to student questions or concerns—will be difficult.

2. Set ground rules for posting and commenting before the activity begins. For example, explain that while humor and creativity are appreciated, offensiveness will result in a grade deduction.

3. Encourage students to tag their blog posts. Tags can catalogue the vocabulary words in specific, meaningful groupings.

4. Consider requiring students, each time they do this activity, to comment on two or three of their classmates' blog posts. Commenting can increase students' personal investment in the blog. It can also foster a stronger sense of community outside of the classroom.

5. If smartphones are unavailable, students can use digital cameras and a computer with an Internet connection.

REFERENCES AND FURTHER READING

Godwin-Jones, R. (2011). Emerging technologies: Mobile apps for language learning. *Language Learning & Technology, 15*, 2–11.

Levy, M. (2009). Technologies in use for second language learning. *Modern Language Journal, 93*, 769–782. doi:10.1111/j.1540-4781.2009.00972.x

Wong, L. H., Chin, C. K., Tan, C. L., & Liu, M. (2010). Students' personal and social meaning making in a Chinese idiom mobile learning environment. *Educational Technology & Society, 13*, 15–26.

V

Smartphone Vocabulary Practice

Mike Misner

Levels	*Any*
Aims	*Use ubiquitous multimodal resources for English language learning*
Class Time	*15 minutes*
Preparation Time	*5 minutes*
Resources	*White board, markers or projector screen, projector, and PowerPoint page*

Students have electronic dictionaries that will give the word for word translation, but using online English language resources such as image searches may lead students to read more about the target vocabulary items on sites such as Wikipedia and others.

PROCEDURE

1. Place students in small groups of three or four.

2. Write or project on the board a set of 6–10 target vocabulary items that students do not yet know well enough. (The words can come from students' previous vocabulary tests, vocabulary journals, difficult words from their intensive reading passages, graded readers, etc. The words can be chosen by either you or students.)

3. Have the groups enter the words in an English language web image search (e.g., Google Images) and save the images to their image galleries on their electronic devices. Alternatively, students can take a picture of the image displayed on another electronic device, using a smartphone or camera.

4. Students then rename their images with the English word, first language (L1) translation, second language (L2) definition, and an original sentence in context.

5. If the above electronic version does not work, have students make a list on a piece of notebook paper of the English word, L1 translation, L2 definition, a quick sketch or pasted image, and an original sentence in context.

6. In pairs, have students do a point-and-say activity with a partner (A points, and B says the English word for the item).

7. Students then switch roles.

8. Have students write a dialogue using the words from the vocabulary list.

9. Using several pictures from their vocabulary lists, students think up/write original stories and tell/read them to each other.

10. They then switch partners and retell the same story with the same pictures.

11. They then switch pictures and tell a new story with the new pictures.

12. They then switch partners again and tell the new story again.

CAVEATS AND OPTIONS

1. An original sentence in context must have the target vocabulary items and an explanation that makes them quite clear.

    - X: I ate the *persimmon*.

    - P: I ate the red soft round *persimmon* with a spoon.

2. Students follow the pictures in the image search back to the website where the pictures were originally posted. Then they read that page and any other linked pages that are interesting. Students do this for several images. The primary purpose is to deepen and contextualize knowledge of the target vocabulary items by finding those items in several helpful contexts. The secondary purpose is to familiarize students with strategies that they can use anytime for their own language learning needs.

3. Using a free web hosting site like Weebly, students make alphabetized or thematic entries with vocabulary words, translations, definitions, image search pictures, sentences in context, and links to articles with the target vocabulary items. The purpose of this online vocabulary journal is to have a list, tailored to students' needs, that can easily be accessed anytime, anywhere, and shared by all students in the class.

4. A large number of flash card applications are available on laptops, tablets, and smartphones. Some of these applications are for babies (e.g., Sound Touch Interactive), and others are for university students (e.g., Dictionary.com

V

Flashcards). Some are free, and others are paid. Most of them have a preset number of words across a limited number of semantic fields, while some others allow you to create your own cards based on your personal language learning needs. Students can use their smartphones to take photos of target vocabulary items in the language learner's environment. The photos can be labeled with the English word, L1 translation, definition, and a sentence in context.

5. Quizlet.com has, among other learning tools, flash cards and vocabulary games such as Race and Scatter.

Using VoiceThread to Promote Vocabulary Learning

Preeya Reddy and Amanda Radwan

Levels	*Pre-intermediate to upper intermediate*
Aims	*Create a vocabulary log*
	Use target vocabulary in context
Class Time	*30–45 minutes*
Preparation Time	*10 minutes*
Resources	*iPads with VoiceThread app*

PROCEDURE

1. Download VoiceThread, an app that allows students to upload images/text and add their voice to it. It promotes collaboration though sharing images, text, and audio recording. It also promotes vocabulary development and oral expression.

2. Pick a theme for students to work on or that is already planned for the class (e.g., jobs).

3. Get students to work on their iPads to collect photos that are related to the theme and save them in their camera library.

4. Show students how to use VoiceThread by helping them sign in and create their account.

5. Have them add their photos and text under each photo. They can also record themselves saying the target word for pronunciation purposes.

6. Higher level students can extend themselves by creating a dialogue between two or more students.

7. They can share their VoiceThread with their classmates, and each one can add more text or comments.

CAVEATS AND OPTIONS

1. Students can also use VoiceThread as a dictation tool. One student can record himself or herself speaking and then type in the word or sentence after listening to it. The student can send this to other students in the group. These students can add to the vocabulary and add their own voices as well.

2. Students can create part of a story or sentences using the target vocabulary, then pass it on via VoiceThread for their peers to contribute and check.

3. You need to have an Internet connection while using VoiceThread. Every user also needs to register and create an account before using the app.

Quizlet for Learning Words and Phrases

Helen Howarth

Levels	*All*
Aims	*Learn, revise, and test vocabulary*
Class Time	*15 minutes*
Preparation Time	*30 minutes*

PROCEDURE

1. Sign up for Quizlet (http://quizlet.com). Quizlet is a free website that enables learners to learn vocabulary using the flashcard or spaced retrieval method as well as enjoy a variety of game-like activities to reinforce and self-test learning. Students learn visually, aurally, and productively.

2. Create your word list by entering words and their definitions into the programme. You can use a good learners' dictionary for this purpose, but it is also possible to select definitions from previous contributors to Quizlet. Pictures can be included.

3. Students can now access this information online. Give them either the link to the word list or the actual name of the list. They can also download the smartphone app.

4. Students can now read, listen to, and learn the words—the spoken language is North American English. They can then consolidate their learning by using a range of games and activities on the website. Explore the website for yourself to see the possibilities.

5. Word lists can also be printed as word cards which enable in-class activities for revision or can be used to pair students for other activities.

CAVEATS AND OPTIONS

1. Quizlet can also be used for learning phrases or collocations. Enter the word alongside one or more useful collocations for that word. At the time of writing, the following websites are very useful for providing frequent collocations: www.just-the-word.com and http://flax.nzdl.org. This enables the collocation to be learnt visually, aurally, and with the correct family word. However, to test knowledge of the collocation, a second version of the collocation list is required. To do this, blank out the target word.

     Example: role: play a _____ in

                         a key _____

2. Make sure students know that the term and definition should not be on the same page. If they do appear on the same page, look at the settings on the right-hand side and click "Start with definition." This is important in order to have spaced retrieval. Note that cards can also be shuffled.

Vocabulary Concordances in the Cloud

Michael Madson

Levels	*Any*
Aims	*Expand vocabulary*
	Increase awareness of sociopragmatic features and contexts
Class Time	*20–30 minutes*
Preparation Time	*10–20 minutes*
Resources	*Computers with Internet connection*
	An account with a cloud computing application, such as Google Docs or Dropbox

There are many cloud computing applications, but those that allow for group document building are best for this activity.

PROCEDURE

1. Compile a list of vocabulary relevant to student interests and needs. The vocabulary might be, for example, headwords from the Academic Word List (Coxhead, 2000), action verbs, or transitions for writing and speaking. At beginning levels, assign one vocabulary word per student. At more advanced levels, assign two to five per student.

2. Grant students access to the cloud computing application such as Google Docs or Dropbox.

3. Have students find sentences for their assigned words from authentic sources, such as websites or magazines, and upload the sentences to the cloud, where the whole class can see them. The concordance is complete when each word on the vocabulary list has 15 sentences. For example, if a student is assigned the word *hinge*, the example sentences might include "The hinge on the door broke" and "Our victory hinges on the team captain."

V

4. Ask students to determine meanings for each word in the concordance. To guide them, you might ask questions such as "In what situations does the word appear?" "Are there multiple meanings, and if so, what are they?" "What is the level of formality?" and "Do other words tend to collocate with the vocabulary?"

5. Have students share their findings in small groups, writing down new insights from other students' findings. At more advanced levels, they might also prepare conference papers or formal reports.

6. Quiz students on the vocabulary, as necessary. Help them reflect on their learning, and provide additional opportunities for them to use their new vocabulary in speaking and writing activities.

7. As appropriate, create a new concordance in the cloud (or expand the existing one) and start again!

CAVEATS AND OPTIONS

1. Students at more advanced levels can develop their own vocabulary lists, tailored to their personal goals, and compile corpora on their own. They might then present these corpora projects to the rest of the class.

2. For students who might struggle with finding authentic sources, the Corpus of Contemporary American English or the Michigan Corpus of Academic Spoken English, both available online, might be helpful. Students can either upload sentences from these corpora or simply determine the meanings of each word.

3. Dictionaries need not be banned; if students use them, they might evaluate the dictionary definitions in light of the corpus, look for collocations, and analyze the vocabulary context and level of formality.

REFERENCES AND FURTHER READING

Corpus of Contemporary American English: http://corpus.byu.edu/coca

Michigan Corpus of Academic Spoken English: http://quod.lib.umich.edu/m/micase

Coxhead, A. (2000). A new academic word list. *TESOL Quarterly, 34*(2), 213–238.

McCarten, J. (2007). *Teaching vocabulary: Lessons from the corpus, lessons for the classroom*. Cambridge, England: Cambridge University Press.

Fill in the Gaps

Tom Cobb

Levels	Intermediate +
Aims	Meet recently learned words in several new contexts in a game environment
Class Time	20 minutes
Preparation Time	20–30 minutes
Resources	List of 20–30 recently studied words
	Computers with Internet access

PROCEDURE

1. Prepare a set of about 20 words that have been recently introduced but are not yet well known. Students will need to (a) reinforce their current knowledge of the words and (b) expand it to include new shades of meaning, contextualized uses, and collocates.

2. Go to the Compleat Lexical Tutor website (www.lextutor.ca) and click the "I-D word" link. Once on the I-D Word page, look at how the demos work and at the corpora available. Press "Submit" with some of the options available to familiarize yourself with the activity.

3. The basic task is to look at the gapped concordance lines and come up with a word that fits all of the contexts (Appendix A). The answer is hidden in the letter string above the gapped lines. Use the computer mouse to highlight the answer. When you answer correctly, the answer appears in the gaps (Appendix B).

4. When you are ready to build the activity for students, the game builder will take the words you provide and create a game asking students to match words hidden in random jumbles of letters to gapped lines. The lines come from the corpus you designate (either graded or academic, depending on students' level).

5. There are some user options such as a new randomized set of gapped concordance lines for any words that are "stuck." Also, a switch makes it possible to either move to the next word immediately or allow a moment of contemplation once the concordance is filled in. The extra time gives students time

to notice interesting collocations like *recover his composure, recover some of the losses,* and *recover his senses* in the example in Appendix B.

6. The game offers cumulative scoring, which makes it suitable to playing competitively.

7. The game can be saved to the Compleat Lexical Tutor site under the name you have chosen. It can then be used in a lab, on a classroom computer, or at home. Learners can be shown how to build and save their own personalized versions of the game.

8. In a lab, one idea is for students to work in pairs or small groups at computers. After each student has had a chance to practice, they can take turns working on increasing their accuracy. This has the advantage that as students work to obtain better scores, they will encounter the words in more new contexts.

9. Once all students have had a chance to improve, a winner can be declared.

CAVEATS AND OPTIONS

1. Select a corpus that is suited to students' proficiency level. They need to be able to understand most if not all of the concordance lines. The graded corpus offers comprehensible contexts suitable for less advanced learners.

2. Once you have built the game, try it in advance of making it available to students. Since the corpora the game draws on are fairly small, it cannot be guaranteed that there will be multiple gapped lines for every word. The game can run with just a few examples, but fewer than four is not ideal. If there are too few lines, try choosing other words or other forms of the target words (e.g., *recovers* instead of *recover*) or selecting a more advanced corpus.

3. As students continue to play, they may bypass examining the gapped lines and just look for familiar forms in the letter strings. To focus their attention on the information in the concordance lines, make a worksheet with questions or tasks such as the following:

   • What do you notice about the grammar of the word? Is it a noun, verb, adjective, or adverb?

   • What is the main meaning of the word in the gapped lines? Does it have other meanings? Explain using examples.

   • Write a sentence using the word and its most frequent collocate.

4. An advantage of this game is that while playing, learners are acquiring skills that will be useful in other tasks involving computer concordancing.

REFERENCES AND FURTHER READING

Cobb, T. (1999). Breadth and depth of lexical acquisition with hands-on concordancing. *Computer Assisted Language Learning, 12,* 345–360. doi:10.1076/call.12.4.345.5699

Parise, P. (n.d.). Student reactions to concordance data: A task using I-D word identification [Web log post]. Retrieved from http://tesolpeter.wordpress.com/student-reactions-to-concordance-dataa-task-using-i-d-word-identification

APPENDIX A: *The Question* *(based on an Academic Word List word)*

sdorrecoverzshv

1. and individuals in an attempt to _____ some of the losses it has suffered

2. the shape of Grattan, has failed to _____ from the travails of last year's portal

3. it is probable that Biggs will never _____ from the beating he took from Tyson.

4. they had done in their attempt to _____ Cyrus Harding. He and Neb had

5. the electrical commotions, could not _____ its former purity, and there was almost

6. anxiety for several days, began to _____ . His constitution brought him through,

7. greedily. "You think that he will _____ his senses?" asked Pencroft. "It is not

8. that wretched man! How he labored to _____ himself by work! How he prayed

9. the light of the sun, he might perhaps _____ ." No, Pencroft, " answered the engineer,"

10. putted out, giving Palmer a chance to _____ his composure, which he had quite visibly

11. age of them. The best course is to _____ his physical excitement by a change of

APPENDIX B: *The Answer*

Recover

1. and individuals in an attempt to RECOVER some of the losses it has suffered

2. the shape of Grattan, has failed to RECOVER from the travails of last year's portal

3. it is probable that Biggs will never RECOVER from the beating he took from Tyson.

4. they had done in their attempt to RECOVER Cyrus Harding. He and Neb had

5. by the electrical commotions, could not RECOVER its former purity, and there was

6. anxiety for several days, began to RECOVER. His constitution brought him through,

7. it greedily. "You think that he will RECOVER his senses?" asked Pencroft. "It is not

8. that wretched man! How he labored to RECOVER himself by work! How he prayed

9. the light of the sun, he might perhaps RECOVER ." No, Pencroft, "answered the

10. putted out, giving Palmer a chance to RECOVER his composure, which he had quite

11. age of them. The best course is to RECOVER his physical excitement by a change of

Computer-Assisted Text Selection

Tom Cobb

Levels	*All*
Aims	*Find out your learners' vocabulary size*
	Select texts for extensive and intensive reading
Class Time	*20–40 minutes*
Preparation Time	*55 minutes*
Resources	*Computer with Internet access*
	Selection of texts in digital format

PROCEDURE

1. Have learners take the Vocabulary Size Test (Nation & Beglar, 2007), which determines their rough vocabulary size. The test can be found on the Compleat Lexical Tutor website: www.lextutor.ca/tests/levels/recognition /1_14k. It can be administered on paper or online.

2. After scoring the test and analysing the results, gather a collection of reading materials for learners in digital format. Open the Compleat Lexical Tutor program Vocabprofile (an adaptation of Nation & Heatley, 1994, available at http://lextutor.ca/vp/bnc) and paste the first text into the input box. Once you click the "Submit" button, the program will analyse the vocabulary components of the text using the 1,000-word frequency levels. Proceed in the same way for each of the other texts.

3. Each text can thus be matched for lexical compatibility with learners' vocabulary size scores. For instance, if learners have a vocabulary size of 3,000 words, then texts made up entirely of 1,000 items will be too easy for them, while texts with a sizable proportion of 3,000- to 5,000-level items will be too difficult. Texts with 85% first-thousand items and about 10% second-thousand items should be about right.

4. Research shows that for comfortable, extensive reading, about 95%–98% of vocabulary items should be familiar, while for intensive reading 90%–95% should be familiar. Little is accomplished when learners read texts with less than 90% of items familiar (the remaining 10% amounts to one unfamiliar word in ten or about one unfamiliar word per line).

5. Gradually a bank of texts can be built up at different levels. A set of example texts with smoothly differentiated profiles can be seen at www.lextutor.ca/vp/bnc/samples.html.

6. Ensure that students select texts from your bank of texts that suit their purpose, depending on whether it is for extensive or intensive reading.

CAVEATS AND OPTIONS

1. Lexis is not the only thing that determines the readability of a text (although it is probably the most important factor). Also important are topic interest and familiarity, sentence length, presence or lack of illustrations, and writing style.

2. Proper nouns will be classified as "difficult words" by Vocabprofile, whereas in fact, learners have no trouble with them. The program offers a check option to reclassify proper nouns as first-thousand (i.e., familiar) items.

3. You may want not just to find texts that match learners' level but also or instead to create or modify existing texts to make them fit learners' level(s). Vocabprofile offers an Edit-To-A-Profile facility.

REFERENCES AND FURTHER READING

Cobb, T. (2007). Computing the vocabulary demands of L2 reading. *Language Learning & Technology, 11*(3), 38–63.

Nation, I. S. P., & Beglar, D. (2007). A vocabulary size test. *The Language Teacher, 31*(1), 9–13.

Nation, I. S. P., & Heatley, A. (1994). *Vocabulary profile and range: Programs for the analysis of vocabulary in texts.* Available from http://www.victoria.ac.nz/lals/about/staff/paul-nation

Schmitt, N., Jiang, X., & Grabe, W. (2010). The percentage of words known in a text and reading comprehension. *Modern Language Journal, 95*(1), 26–43. doi:10.1111/j.1540-4781.2011.01146.x

Read It, Hear It, Look It Up

Tom Cobb

Levels	*Intermediate +*
Aims	*Develop skills for reading texts outside the comfort zone*
Class Time	*40 minutes*
Preparation Time	*20 minutes*
Resources	*Computers with Internet access*

PROCEDURE

1. Find a text of 500–1,000 words that learners want or need to comprehend but that goes a bit beyond their comfort level. (See the activity "Computer-Assisted Text Selection" in this section to find such a text.)

2. Go to the Compleat Lexical Tutor website (www.lextutor.ca) and click the "Hypertext" link, choosing Hypertext 2. To become familiar with the activity, play with the demo texts provided on the input page, clicking them into the box and clicking "Build" to create Hypertext pages.

3. The Hypertext format offers two support options: You can click on any word to hear it pronounced, and you can obtain a clear, ad-free definition (in an education-friendly version kindly provided by Wordreference.com). The definition appears in an independent space on the screen.

4. Once you feel familiar with the tools, type or paste the text that learners will work with into the box and give it a short, memorable name. Next, choose a suitable dictionary from the menu, either the Wordreference monolingual option or one of its 12 bilingual dictionaries. Then click "Build."

5. When the page appears, check its format and functionality before clicking "Save on Lextutor as . . ." (+ the name that was given in Step 4). This produces the URL that learners will use to access the page.

6. Students work alone or in pairs to read the text, listening to and looking up words as needed. Look-ups are recorded in a space at the top of the text and in a cumulative file that you can access.

7. A number of follow-ups are possible, including sending the looked-up words to one of the Compleat Lexical Tutor's other learning activities (for example, see the activity "Fill in the Gaps" in this section of the book).

CAVEATS AND OPTIONS

1. A "Finished Reading" button appears on the students' text. Clicking on it reveals a list of the words selected for look-up and listening. This feature could be used by learners to keep a record of their new words or by you to determine how students are using this resource. No look-ups could indicate the text is not challenging enough. Too many look-ups could indicate the text is too difficult or that learners need help in determining which words are important to look up. One response to too many look-ups is to impose a time limit for the reading.

2. If the text has an equivalent sound file, such as those provided by Voice of America (www.voanews.com), this can be included to create a read-while-listening version of Hypertext.

3. Comprehension can be tested by putting the same text or a summary of it into the Clozebuilder (available at the Compleat Lexical Tutor site). This software produces a cloze passage of the text in a format suitable for printing or as an online version (with a "Save" feature leading to a URL, as described above).

4. The online dictionary makes look-ups efficient. It avoids the usual problem of paper dictionaries, which is that the look-ups take readers away from the text for a long time—so long that they may disengage with the message of the text. Similarly, the listing function of the "Finished Reading" feature should reduce the time away from the text for learners who want to copy their new words down. They can simply collect them at the end.

5. Use of Hypertext can help learners build vocabulary and develop strategies for intensive reading. It is also good preparation for navigating other types of interactive documents that now often include click-on definitions, and other resources, such as PDFs and smartphones.

REFERENCES AND FURTHER READING

Cobb, T. (2006). Internet and literacy in the developing world: Delivering the teacher with the text. *Educational Technology Research & Development, 54,* 627–645.

Cobb, T., Greaves, C., & Horst, M. (2001). Can the rate of lexical acquisition from reading be increased? An experiment in reading French with a suite of on-line resources. In P. Raymond & C. Cornaire (Eds.), *Regards sur la didactique des langues secondes* (pp. 133–153). Montréal, Quebec, Canada: Éditions Logique.

V

Select and Recall Vocabulary From Digital Games

Julie Bytheway

Levels	*Multilevel*
Aims	*Be aware of explicit vocabulary selection and learning in digital games*
	Use recall to remember and learn vocabulary
Class Time	*20 minutes*
Preparation Time	*None*
Resources	*Access to digital games through smartphones, computers, or gaming consoles*

PROCEDURE

1. To set up the activity, ask learners to brainstorm all the digital games they have heard about. If learners are not familiar with digital games, have them use online search engines to identify popular digital games.

2. Tell learners to sort the games into categories, such as free/paid, platforms/consoles/devices (e.g., Mac, PC, Xbox, PS, Wii, DS, iOS, Android), and game type (e.g., word games, trivia games, card games, racing games, real-time strategy games, construction simulations, MMORPGs, graphic adventures, first-person shooter games, platform fantasy games, maze games, puzzle games).

3. Discuss with learners how to select useful words to learn. Encourage them to select words that are repeated, used frequently, and can be used in other contexts.

4. For homework, tell learners to play digital games of their choice in English on a console or device they have access to. Tell them to ensure the game's or gaming device's language settings are set to English.

5. Ask learners to select two useful words to learn from a digital game every day. They do not write the words down; they just remember the words.

6. Tell learners to recall their two words intermittently throughout the day, every day. Suggest that they recall by purposefully remembering the two

words when they do something like walk up or down stairs, put their phone in or out of their pocket, or open or close their bag.

7. During the next class, have learners walk around the classroom and tell at least three people which two words they selected, explaining how the words are used in different contexts (and listen to three people too). You can join in this activity. Do this activity when your group needs a 5-minute energizing break.

8. Repeat this activity every lesson for at least 3 months because repetition is needed to build up a useful quantity of vocabulary and make word selection, repeated word recall, and word learning useful habits.

CAVEATS AND OPTIONS

1. When increasing learners' responsibility for learning and using digital games as a language learning function, you may need to explain and justify the value of the learning tasks to learners, parents, colleagues, and administrators.

2. Learners may want to select many words during each session of game play, but encourage just a few words so that learners can recall them easily. Long lists of words learned hurriedly are more likely to be forgotten. A few words often may be more useful over the long term.

3. Playing digital games may not be attractive to all learners, but it may be highly motivating to other learners who may not enjoy more traditional forms of passive media.

4. Encourage learners to select vocabulary from other sources in the real and digital worlds around them (e.g., television, news articles, comic books, conversations).

5. Ask learners to purposefully use words they have selected and learned from digital games in classroom speaking and writing activities.

6. At the end of every week (or series of lessons), have learners move around the room and recommend to other learners two or three words that they think are extremely useful. Learners then select two or three words from the recommendations to recall and remember.

7. In small groups, learners can discuss and evaluate the range and usefulness of vocabulary available in a variety of digital games.

8. In small groups, learners can make posters to display on the classroom wall explaining how digital games can help vocabulary learning, including examples of specific games and vocabulary.

V

Collaborative Vocabulary Review With Padlet

Dinah Ouano Perren

Levels	*Intermediate +*
Aims	*Reinforce previously learned vocabulary by using technology*
Class Time	*10–15 minutes*
Preparation Time	*15 minutes*
Resources	*Website www.padlet.com with teacher's account*
	Mobile devices (smartphones, tablets, iPads, laptops, etc.)
	Internet access
	Screen and projector or a document imager for viewing results

This activity allows you to reinforce previously learned vocabulary by using technology to review and assess student-generated sentences more effectively during class (compared to handwritten methods). Preparation in advance allows for instantaneous real-time effect during class. Although there are several steps to get started, set-up time decreases once you are familiar with the procedure. Allow 2–3 minutes to create a Padlet account online (one time only), then 5–10 minutes to create a Padlet link and then email it to the intended students. A new link will have to be made each time you do this activity.

PROCEDURE

Before Class

1. Go to www.padlet.com to log in and then click "Build a Wall." This wall will be the canvas on which students will type their sentences.

2. Next, click "Modify Wall" to add a title and a description. Since the purpose of this activity is reviewing words on a regular basis, the title can be the current date and/or textbook chapter. You can choose how you want to word the description, which is basically a simple instruction for students to

produce their own sentences (e.g., *Write a sentence using a new vocabulary word from page 27, Type your group # and sentence now*).

3. You can also choose to add wallpaper and a small image (called a portrait). These options are useful for identification purposes, for example, when using Padlet for more than one class. Also, the result is more visually appealing.

4. A unique address/URL is automatically created each time you build a wall; copy this URL and email it to students.

In Class

Students work in small groups with the goal of generating one sentence that contains correct usage of a vocabulary word. You can give the same word to all groups or assign a different word for each group. Students discuss and agree on the sentence together, but only one student from each group types their sentence on the Padlet website.

1. Set up your computer and projector so that you can view students' progress in real time.

2. Place students into groups of three or four; assign a group name or number. Announce how much time they have to complete the task.

3. Make sure at least one person in the group can access the Internet with a mobile device.

4. Ask the students using a mobile device to open the link you sent via email. It is best to have only one typist per group so that the focus is on creating a new sentence together using speaking and listening skills.

5. When students open the link, they will see the wall you created with your instructions. To begin typing, students double-click anywhere on the wall and a small white dialogue box will appear.

6. Have students place the cursor next to "Your Name/Post Title" and then type in their group name or number (this will appear in red). Have them place the cursor next to "Write something . . . ." This area is where they will type the sentence they create as a group. Remind group members to check the sentence for grammar, spelling, punctuation, and so on. After each group types their sentence, clicking anywhere on the wallpaper outside of the white box will complete their activity and edits can no longer be made.

7. While students are working on their sentences, you can circulate around the room to monitor progress. Once all the groups have completed the activity, or when time is up, tell the class to focus on the screen/monitor to view their work. As a whole class, review each generated sentence for assessment.

V

CAVEATS AND OPTIONS

1. If class size is small, this activity can be completed individually as long as each student has a mobile device.

2. Student groups can assess another group's sentence and then retype with revisions.

3. Explain to students how using Padlet relates specifically to the *TESOL Technology Standards* for English language learners (Healey et al., 2011).

REFERENCES AND FURTHER READING

Healey, D., Hanson-Smith, E., Hubbard, P., Ioannou-Georgiou, S., Kessler, G., & Ware, P. (2011). *TESOL technology standards: Description, implementation, integration.* Alexandria, VA: TESOL.

Vocabulary, Revision, and Growth Online

Haidee Thomson

Levels	**All**
Aims	**Revise new vocabulary and phrases from class receptively and productively**
Class Time	**10 minutes**
Preparation Time	**10 minutes**
Resources	**Computer with Internet connection**

PROCEDURE

1. Before class, take a list of words or phrases that learners need to revise and enter them into the free online program Memrise (www.memrise.com). The program provides a game-like environment for revision.

   a. Set up a username and password, then scroll down and click the "+Create a Course" button.

   b. Select the language you are teaching and the students' first language, and give the course a name.

   c. Click "Create Course."

   d. Add target items and first language (L1) equivalents.

   e. Click "Advanced" and "Add column."

   f. Name the extra column "Example sentence." Enter an example sentence in the new column with a gap for the target word and a hint (L1 equivalent or a synonym) in brackets.

   g. Click on the pencil icon to edit "Test on English, prompt with context sentence."

   h. When you have entered the target items, click "Details" tab and change the status of the course to "unlisted" and save it, which privately publishes your course while also allowing you to continue adding to it.

   i. Check what students will see by clicking "Start planting."

2. In class, share the web address of your course and ask students to sign up.

3. Create a memory trigger for each item by clicking "Add a mem." Model this process and elicit ideas from learners so that they understand the concept and process.

4. Select an image from Memrise that connects the new word with existing knowledge so that retrieval becomes easier (see Levin, Levin, Glasman, & Nordwall, 1992).

5. Enter a familiar word onto the image which sounds similar to the target word. For example, a Japanese speaker might choose *ni* (*two*) as a key word for the target word *knee* in English because it sounds similar, even though the meaning is completely different. Click "Save" and "Next."

6. Encourage learners to make their own mems, personalising their associations with the target language. After making mems, learners will be prompted to rehearse target words.

7. Select the target item from multichoice options in response to the context sentence prompt (receptive rehearsal). For phrases, learners must rearrange the words in the correct order.

8. Type the word or phrase in response to the prompt (productive retrieval). Rehearsal/retrieval frequency is automatically adjusted in response to learner progress; as items are correctly answered, the spacing increases.

9. Practise using Memrise in the classroom for about 10 minutes every class. Each learner should use his or her own device (PC or smartphone) at his or her own pace. When learners are familiar and involved with the learning, the program can be set for homework to revise words and phrases covered in class.

10. Set goals for learning measured by growth of seeds into flowers (which represent target items). As rehearsal and accuracy increase, the seeds grow into flowers, which represent known words.

11. Check learner progress and ranking on the Leaderboard, which shows accumulative weekly, monthly, and total scores.

CAVEATS AND OPTIONS

1. Once learners are signed up for a course, the system will automatically send them email reminders to refresh their memories at spaced intervals for maximum retrieval and retention (cf. Hulstijn, 2001, p. 286).

2. Memrise is often updated, so the order of these instructions may change with time; however, editing options are generally clear, and the overarching concept of memory embellishment and spaced rehearsal will still apply.

3. Instead of entering each item separately, there is a "Bulk add items" option in the editing "Advanced" menu where you can paste a word list.

4. Instead of entering all the target words into the program yourself, you can add learners as "contributors" and give them responsibility to add words periodically so that everyone plays an active role in the course.

5. When creating a mem, if similar-sounding familiar words are difficult to find, another option is entering the first letters of the target word with the rest of the word gapped in the mem.

6. This activity is also good for autonomous learning and homework.

REFERENCES AND FURTHER READING

Hulstijn, J. (2001). Intentional and incidental second language vocabulary learning: A reappraisal of elaboration, rehearsal, and automaticity. In P. Robinson (Ed.), *Cognition and second language instruction* (pp. 258–286). Cambridge, England: Cambridge University Press.

Levin, J. R., Levin, M. E., Glasman, L. D., & Nordwall, M. B. (1992). Mnemonic vocabulary instruction: Additional effectiveness evidence. *Contemporary Educational Psychology, 17*(2), 156–174. doi:10.1016/0361-476X(92)90056-5

V

Flip Your Cards and Go With A+ FlashCards Pro

Ida Dolci and Peter Davidson

Levels	Any
Aims	Create and manage personal word banks
	Review lexical items, definitions, and spelling
Class Time	30–45 minutes
Preparation Time	40–45 minutes
Resources	iPad with A+ FlashCards Pro app

A+ FlashCards Pro is a motivating and fun app that helps students review the meaning of lexical items and assists them in learning how to spell and define each word. Parts of speech, voiceover, and images may also be used to enhance the learning process.

PROCEDURE

1. Connect your iPad to a projector (if you have one) to demonstrate how to use A+ FlashCards Pro (see the Appendix).

2. Once the cards are ready, three options will pop up: Know, Not sure, and Don't know.

3. Students flip the cards and then drag them into the correct category. This depends on whether they know the meaning, spelling, and definition of the word.

4. The three categories will "store the cards" for further practice.

5. Students continue to test themselves and each other if they play in a group.

6. Once the game is over, a pop-up will appear to inform students of their progress.

7. At any time during the "testing phase" students can click on the arrow in the right-hand bottom corner. This will provide them with a progress chart.

8. Students can continue to test themselves or each other by referring to their cards with a translation, the image, or recorded voice.

9. Students can edit their cards at any point by simply clicking on "Settings" and then "Edit cards."

CAVEATS AND OPTIONS

For further practice, students can upload the set of cards to the Quizlet app in the "Settings."

APPENDIX: *Preparation*

1. Download the app from the App Store. https://itunes.apple.com/us/app/a+ -flashcards-pro/id395248242?mt=8.

2. Click the + in the top left-hand corner.

3. Create a set of word cards.

4. Choose from the four options available: term (word), term and translation (into a language of choice), term and image, and term and voice.

5. Add a title to the lexical set.

6. Tap the screen to add a new card.

7. Add your word. Then import/draw image, add a definition or translate, and choose your language (see Figure 1).

8. Continue to add cards to create a lexical set.

Figure 1. Examples of drawing and definition

Revise Your Vocabulary With Quizlet

Ida Dolci and Peter Davidson

Levels	Any
Aims	Create and manage personal word banks
	Review lexical items, definitions, and spelling
Class Time	30–45 minutes
Preparation Time	10 minutes
Resources	iPadwith Quizlet app and A+ FlashCards Pro app

Quizlet is a fun way to review, spell, and match definitions. It allows students to work at their own pace and recycle lexis in a motivating and meaningful fashion.

PROCEDURE

1. Download Quizlet from the App Store and register online: https://itunes
   .apple.com/us/app/quizlet/id546473125?mt=8.

2. In A+ FlashCards Pro, prepare vocabulary cards of the lexical items you
   would like to review and then upload them to Quizlet. The number of cards
   you prepare depends on the number of items in your lexical set/unit.

3. Log into Quizlet, follow instructions, and click "Allow."

4. Once you are in the app, you have access to your uploaded vocabulary sets
   from A+ FlashCards Pro. You also have access to your Study Feed and
   Favorites. Click on each option available to track your progress.

5. You can also search for sets of words that other teachers and students have
   created by typing in, in the top left-hand corner of the screen.

Search sets/classes/users

6. Click on a set of cards that you would like to review.

7. Each set has three game options: Cards, Learn, and Scatter. These options allow you to recycle the lexical items in different ways.

8. In Cards mode, click on the card and it will flip to the definition, picture, and/or meaning of the word. This, of course, depends on how the card is created in A+ FlashCards Pro. Click the volume icon in the top right-hand corner to listen to the pronunciation of the word, and click "Pause" when necessary. To change the language to prompt with, click on this icon: ✻.

9. In Learn mode, you spell the word. Click on the ✻ icon to decide which language to play in. You choose which language to prompt with. Then, spell the word on the screen. Click "Go" to submit your answer and check your spelling. Track your progress by referring to the scoring system at the top of the screen.

10. Cheat with your spelling by clicking the "Don't Know" button on the screen, and then try again. If you make a mistake with the spelling of the word, the letters that need changing will appear in red, while those that are correct will be in green. Students can compete against each other if they play in groups in class or try to beat their previous spelling scores.

11. In Scatter mode, you match the words with their definitions. Click on "Start Game" to begin the activity. Tap on a word and its definition. Once the words are matched, they disappear from the screen. There is a timer in the right-hand corner of the screen, which introduces a competitive element, and students play to beat their time. Play Scatter individually, in small groups, or as a whole class (by displaying on a screen through the projector). Repeat to try to beat the previous timing.

CAVEATS AND OPTIONS

1. Do not include parts of speech in the creation of the cards. If you do, the pronunciation feature in Cards mode will not function correctly.

2. Talk with learners about ways to bring this vocabulary work into their language use.

Rapid Reaction

Marlise Horst and Tom Cobb

Levels	*Any*
Aims	*Develop the ability to make rapid form–meaning connections*
Class Time	*20 minutes*
Preparation Time	*20–30 minutes*
Resources	*List of 20–30 recently studied words*
	Computers with Internet access

PROCEDURE

1. You will need a set of about 20 words that differ on a basic semantic feature (e.g., living vs. nonliving, pleasant vs. unpleasant, edible vs. nonedible, verb vs. noun). The set should be more or less evenly divided. Thus if the choice is edible vs. nonedible, there should be about 10 edible and 10 nonedible items.

2. Go the Compleat Lexical Tutor website (www.lextutor.ca) and click the "RT Builder" link. Once on the RT page, select the "(In)Animacy" demo to see a model of the reaction time (RT) game you will build for students (see Appendix). Try it and click to see your reaction time results. The goal is to be both accurate (verify that all answers are OK) and fast (note the mean RT and try to improve on it in the next round).

3. Now return to the RT page and build your own activity by rewriting the question in the question box to fit your 20 words. For example, if you are using an edible vs. nonedible distinction, the question will read, "Is it something you can eat?" The instructions will also need to be adjusted to fit: "If it is something you can eat, type 1 for yes" and "If it is something you cannot eat, type 3 for no."

4. The next step is to enter the 10 yes and 10 no words into appropriate boxes. Then when you click "Build it," a new RT game using your question, instructions, and vocabulary should appear. Be sure to try the activity before you click the "Save as" option.

5. By clicking "Save as," you save the activity at a link that you can share with students. You may also wish to create and save a small demo version.

6. In the computer lab, show students how the game works using your demo or the "(In)Animacy" demo available at the Compleat Lexical Tutor.

7. Students work in pairs or small groups at computers. After each student has had a chance to practice, they can take turns working on increasing their accuracy and lowering their times. Each student will need several tries.

8. Once all students have had a chance to improve, a winner can be declared.

CAVEATS AND OPTIONS

1. Prepare several RT games for use in the same session, each with a different semantic distinction. Some of the vocabulary used in one game can be used again in a different way in another game.

2. Students can be shown how use the tools at the Compleat Lexical Tutor site to make their own RT games to share with classmates.

REFERENCES AND FURTHER READING

Cobb, T., & Horst, M. (2011). Does *Word Coach* coach words? *CALICO Journal, 28*, 639–661.

V

APPENDIX: *Compleat Lexical Tutor Reaction Time Builder With Sample Animate and Inanimate Words*

Home>RT Builder

Complete Reaction Timer v.4.5

To build timed language processing instruments, with or without priming

Learners/subjects make timed choices about which of two categories a word or larger unit belongs in (real word or nonword, animate or inanimate, same or different, correct or incorrect, known or unknown, etc.).

1. **Formulate the choice as a Yes-No Question**

2. **Load inputs**

    Tell Ss the question and how to answer it (see Demos =>)

    QUESTION: Do these words refer to something animate (living)?

    INSTRUCTIONS: Type 2 to start. Wait.

    When a word appears in the yellow box:

    If it refers to something animate, type 1 for Yes.

    Put **Yes** words here (Ss type "1" to answer <u>Yes</u> to these words).

    fish snake dog cat bird heart mother girlfriend

    Put **No** words here (Ss type "3" to answer <u>No</u> to these words).

    table road pole carpet glass dirt metal shoe pillow

3. **Try it.**

Type 2 for Start....

    With fingers over 1, 2, & 3—

    Type 1 for YES, 3 for NO.

    Type 2 for NEXT WORD.

Pic Collage

Preeya Reddy and Peter Davidson

Levels	**Beginner to intermediate**
Aims	**Create personal word banks to learn and remember new words**
Class time	**30–45 minutes**
Preparation Time	**None**
Resources	**iPad with Pic Collage app**

Pic Collage is a bright and colorful way for students to personalize and use new vocabulary.

PROCEDURE

1. Connect your iPad to a projector (if you have one), to demonstrate how to use Pic Collage to the class (available at https://itunes.apple.com/app /id448639966).

2. Show students how to take and insert new photos from the camera roll or web. Tools you could use include adding a background, frame, text, and stickers.

3. Give students sufficient time to take photos using their iPads to illustrate the vocabulary that they are learning, or collect images off the web.

4. Have students arrange the pictures and add text to illustrate them. Lower-level students can write the words below the pictures. Higher-level students can write sentences under the pictures to illustrate key vocabulary in context (10–15 words fit in nicely with each Pic Collage).

5. Students can send their Pic Collages to you by email, or their iPad screens can be projected in class, to share their work. See the Appendix for two example Pic Collages.

V

CAVEATS AND OPTIONS

1. Students can create one-word posters, and these can be printed in color and displayed around the classroom.

2. Students who find it useful to translate words in their first language can also write the word in their L1 alongside the English translation and add a picture to help them learn the target word.

3. Pic Collage allows access to pictures from the web. To prevent students from accessing inappropriate material, it is best to have Wi-Fi switched off and ask (especially younger) students to take their own pictures using the camera on the iPad. These pictures are then stored on their camera roll and can be accessed via Pic Collage.

APPENDIX: *Two Example Pic Collages*

Vocabulary for Specific Purposes

- **Making Decisions on Specialized Vocabulary**

- **Using Specialized Vocabulary**

Part VI: Vocabulary for Specific Purposes

he final part of this book looks at vocabulary for specific purposes, meaning lexical items that are used in specialized subject areas. These specialized words and multiword units tend to appear in one subject area and have a technical meaning which learners need to know. An example of a specialised word in teaching is *pedagogy*, which does not tend to occur in texts in other fields. Specialized vocabulary is important for several reasons. First, it is likely to represent a fairly large proportion of the text. According to Chung and Nation (2003), it could account for up to 30% of the total number of words in a specialized text. The degree of specificity of a text or a subject can affect the degree of technicality of the language in the text. Basturkmen (2010) describes this varying degree of specificity as being a continuum. General vocabulary tends to occur in a wide range of texts, whereas more specialized vocabulary is less likely to occur in a variety of texts. For example, we tend to see *photosynthesis* in particular texts. Unless we work in horticulture or agricultural research, for example, we would not see that word in everyday reading or hear it in everyday conversations.

Another interesting point about specialized vocabulary is that some general words can take on specialized meanings in particular subject areas. Think about *weight,* for example. In physics, it has a particular meaning, just as *accurate* and *precise* have specialized meanings in physics. It can be tricky for learners to develop their understanding of the specialized meaning of a general word because they may think they already know the word and not recognize that it has a more specific meaning in a particular subject area. Another difficulty is that learners might not encounter these words in any other part of their lives, which means they do not get the opportunity to benefit from repetitions or to talk about the words and become comfortable with using them in speaking and writing. It is not just second and foreign language learners who might struggle with specialized vocabulary. Native speakers in secondary schools and in university studies also have a great deal of learning to do in this area. See Coxhead (2012) for more on specialized vocabulary learning and teaching in secondary schools. This need for specialized vocabulary does not stop with secondary or university education. It generally continues as learners encounter specialized vocabulary in their workplaces as well.

This part of the book is divided into two main sections. The first is on making decisions on specialized vocabulary. It presents several ways to decide which words might be specialized for learners as well as ways to focus on these lexical items (single-word and multiword units) in class. The second section presents ways to have learners use specialized vocabulary in their speaking and writing as well as to work with them in reading and listening. You can see from this section that the four strands (Nation, 2007) are at play here again, but this time with more specialized vocabulary. For more on using the four strands as part of a course on science-specific vocabulary, see Hirsh and Coxhead (2009).

REFERENCES

Basturkmen, H. (2010). *Developing courses in English for specific purposes.* Basingstoke, England: Palgrave Macmillan.

Chung, T., & Nation, P. (2003). Technical vocabulary in specialised texts. *Reading in a Foreign Language, 15*(2), 103–116.

Coxhead, A. (2012). Specialised vocabulary in secondary school classrooms: Teachers' perspectives. In H. Pillay & M. Yeo (Eds.), *Teaching language to learners of different age groups* (pp. 194–205). Singapore: SEAMEO Regional Language Centre.

Hirsh, D., & Coxhead, A. (2009). Ten ways of focussing on science-specific vocabulary in EAP. *English Australia Journal, 25*(1), 5–16.

Nation, I. S. P. (2007). The four strands. *Innovation in Language Learning and Teaching, 1*(1), 2–13. doi:10.2167/illt039.0

Identifying Specialised Vocabulary

Averil Coxhead

Levels	*Any*
Aims	*Categorise and define specialised vocabulary*
Class Time	*30 minutes*
Preparation Time	*5 minutes*
Resources	*Scale for reference (Appendix)*

PROCEDURE

1. Discuss the concept of technical or specialised vocabulary with the class. How do learners decide what is a technical word? Do they, for example, consult a dictionary?

2. Introduce Chung and Nation's (2003) scale for identifying technical vocabulary (see the Appendix) as a handout or on screen for the class to see. Discuss the examples from this scale. Note that the example in the Appendix relates to anatomy, but it can be adapted to any subject area or specialisation.

3. Provide some examples of words, and ask the class to decide in small groups or pairs which step on the scale they might belong to.

4. Bring the class back together, and decide on the steps for each of the words.

5. Ask learners to suggest at least three words from their specialised subject area that fit into each of the four steps of the scale. Have them share their examples in small groups.

6. Discuss as a class how this scale might be used in class to decide which words to focus on learning and teaching. Decide on actions to be taken with words from the different steps, for example. If a word is highly technical (Step 4), what should the class do with it? Should they spend time learning it? If it is Step 1, what action should the class take?

7. For subsequent classes, set up a time for a discussion of the words from each class session, what step they belong to on the scale, and therefore what action is to be taken for those words.

VI

CAVEATS AND OPTIONS

1. Consider using a word card system with a vocabulary box for the class to keep track of the technical words from class.

2. Individual class members might want to keep notebooks, electronic word cards, or use other techniques for keeping track of their technical vocabulary. Encourage learners to share ideas about ways to learn specialized vocabulary.

REFERENCES

Chung, T., & Nation, I. S. P. (2003). Technical vocabulary in specialised texts. *Reading in a Foreign Language, 15*(2), 103–116.

APPENDIX: *Chung and Nation's (2003)* Rating Scale for Finding Technical Words as Applied to an Anatomy Text

Step 1

Words such as function words that have a meaning that has no particular relationship with the field of anatomy, that is, words independent of the subject matter.

Examples: *the, is, between, it, by, 12, adjacent, amounts, common, commonly, directly, constantly, early, especially*

Step 2

Words that have a meaning that is minimally related to the field of anatomy in that they describe the positions, movements, or features of the body.

Examples: *superior, part, forms, pairs, structures, surrounds, supports, associated, lodges, protects*

Step 3

Words that have a meaning that is closely related to the field of anatomy. They refer to parts, structures, or functions of the body, such as the regions of the body and systems of the body. Such words are also used in general language. The words may have some restrictions of usage depending on the subject field. Words in this category may be technical terms in a specific field like anatomy and yet may occur with the same meaning in other fields and not be technical terms in those fields.

Examples: *chest, trunk, neck, abdomen, ribs, breast, cage, cavity, shoulder, girdle, skin, muscles, wall, heart, lungs, organs, liver, bony, abdominal, breathing*

Step 4

Words that have a meaning specific to the field of anatomy and are not likely to be known in general language. They refer to structures and functions of the body. These words have clear restrictions of usage depending on the subject field.

Examples: thorax, sternum, costal, vertebrae, pectoral, fascia, trachea, mammary, periosteum, hematopoietic, pectoralis, viscera, intervertebral, demifacets, pedicle

Digital Vocabulary Ethnography

Michael Madson

Levels	*Advanced*
Aims	*Expand vocabulary of particular contexts*
	Engage in individual learning
Class Time	*30–40 minutes*
Preparation Time	*5–20 minutes*
Resources	*Computers with Internet access*
	Audio recorders, if you are planning to have interviews

PROCEDURE

1. Have students reflect on their academic and professional goals, such as through freewriting. For example: What do they want to study? What job do they want? How might English help achieve these goals, and where might they go to learn about them?

2. Explore the importance of academic and professional vocabulary on their goals, and have students brainstorm vocabulary-rich websites and develop research plans. This plan is called their *digital ethnography*. For instance, students interested in technology might explore the vocabulary of websites, user forms, and online videos from Apple or Microsoft. Students interested in studying history might locate historical archives and databases online and study the vocabulary there. At advanced levels, students might consider whom they might interview over Skype or email.

3. Ask students to draft one-page research proposals (see the Appendix). Based on their proposals, offer guidance to strengthen their projects. That guidance might help students write the research proposal in greater clarity and detail, expand (or narrow) the scope of their project, or consider ways of storing and organizing their anticipated data.

4. After the research proposals are approved, have students begin to gather texts and other digital materials from their sites. As they conduct their digital ethnography, have them compile a list of 25–30 important words and phrases, and encourage them to note, in as much detail as they can,

the contexts where these words and phrases are used. The importance of a word or phrase is, of course, subjective. Thus, you might provide criteria to help students think about the word's importance, such as how frequently it appears or how much information it conveys. At more advanced levels, students might brainstorm criteria of their own, which can evolve as the digital ethnographies are carried out.

5. Ask students to share their list of vocabulary findings. Allow class time for presentations or other discussions of their research. Having only one speaker at a time can be tedious, especially in a large class. Consider assigning three or four students to present in each class period, or have students present to each other in small groups.

6. Help students develop personal goals that apply and expand on the vocabulary they learned through their digital ethnography.

CAVEATS AND OPTIONS

1. Some materials might not be suitable for research. For example, materials should, for ethical reasons, be omitted from private discussion boards or interviewees who aren't made aware how their responses will be used. If students struggle with the research proposal, encourage them to visit their research sites and collect some texts. Those texts can help them consider why they chose that site, what writings they might collect, and so on.

2. As digital ethnography can include offline settings, students can also do observations, document collections, and interviews in person.

3. Typically, ethnographers collect data for lengthy periods of time. If students conduct their ethnography over several weeks, ask them to do regular progress reports (see the Appendix) on their research efforts and preliminary findings.

4. Students at very advanced levels might arrange and record interviews and then transcribe them (or parts of them, at least).

REFERENCES AND FURTHER READING

Boellstorff, T., Nardi, B., Pearce, C., & Taylor, T. L. (2012). *Ethnography and virtual worlds: A handbook of method.* Princeton, NJ: Princeton University Press.

VI

APPENDIX: *Research Proposal*

What is your research site, and why?

> *This research site should be a place you are interested in. Describe it in as much detail as you can.*

Where might your observations take place?

> *These observations might be online, in person, or a combination of both.*

Who might you talk to, and how might you talk to them?

> *Consider who is available and knows your research topic well. If you can interview them, how would you do so (email, Skype, mobile phone, etc.)?*

What writings might you collect?

> *These might be sentences on websites, program brochures, YouTube videos, and other digital resources, for example.*

Progress report

Date:

What vocabulary sites have you studied?

How have you studied them?

What have you learned from your research so far?

What help do you need (or would you like)?

Interactive Card Activity for Subject-Specific Vocabulary Collocations

Daniel Hayes, Kimberly Specht, and Andre Scholze

Levels	*Pre-intermediate*
Aims	*Review and maintain new vocabulary in assorted subject-specific settings*
Class Time	*20–30 minutes (weekly, over 4 weeks)*
Preparation Time	*50 minutes*
Resources	*Subject-specific vocational/academic textbook or source*
	Index cards/cardstock
	Whiteboard/chalkboard/flipchart
	Markers/chalk
	Card template (see Appendix)

PROCEDURE

1. Decide what words/phrases to teach and to what category the new words/phrases belong. Each card set contains one category card and six cards containing new words/phrases. With a marker, label each card accordingly (see Appendix). There will be as many card sets as there are categories.

2. Show the class a word card set, and write the category name and the collocation words/phrases on the board. Ask students to find the one word/phrase that does not belong to the content category on the board.

3. Next, divide the class into groups of two or three and distribute one card set to each group. Instruct the groups to identify the category card from the set.

4. Ask each group to write this category name only on the board.

5. Instruct groups to find the card that does not belong in their category. Using the list of categories on the board, students identify the category for the word/phrase card that does not belong in their set.

VI

6. Students from all groups verbally negotiate to place this mismatched word/phrase in the correct category.

7. Check that the card sets have been completed correctly before students present them to the class. If not, Steps 5 and 6 should be repeated. Ask students to copy their words/phrases to their corresponding category on the board.

8. At the end of this activity, have students present their category name and collocation words to the rest of the class.

CAVEATS AND OPTIONS

1. This activity can be easily altered from week to week so that each student group receives a card set with an increasing proportion of mismatched collocation cards, leading to a necessary increase in negotiated interaction with classmates and subsequent review.

2. Higher-level students may begin with a larger number of mismatched collocation cards in Week 1.

3. Depending on the class size, or to increase difficulty, each group can be given more than one card set.

4. Card sets can be adjusted to include more or fewer collocation cards, depending on the students' level.

5. This activity can be used for essential subject-specific vocabulary in a variety of settings, for example, medical staff training (anatomy), technology (flight instruments for pilots), or service industry (flight attendants). Card sets can be adapted in length or complexity to suit the intended setting.

APPENDIX: *Prepared Card Sets*

Note: The mismatched collocation card is <u>underlined</u>.

Respiratory System

Larynx	Trachea

Bronchial Passage	Nasal Passage

Trachea	<u>Heart</u>

Textbook ABCs

Susan L. Schwartz

Levels	*Intermediate +*
Aims	*Reinforce understanding of academic vocabulary*
	Develop study guides for academic subjects
	Practice working cooperatively in groups
Class Time	*10–15 minutes during several class periods*
Preparation Time	*5 minutes*
Resources	*Handout that lists the letters of the alphabet*
	Textbook

PROCEDURE

1. After reading a chapter in a social studies, science, or other academic textbook, give students a handout listing the letters of the alphabet, with space available for writing next to each letter. Tell students they will create an ABC, or alphabet, book about the information in the chapter they just read. (This activity expands the idea of using an ABC handout presented by Jim Cummins at a 2006 workshop in Massachusetts.)

2. Tell students to write words or phrases about the chapter content for each letter of the alphabet: First write the target vocabulary words from the textbook, then fill in the rest of the handout with other words and phrases that address the ideas, people, and events discussed in the chapter. For example, using vocabulary words about the Indus River civilization in Chapter 8 of *Explore the Ancient World* (Langston, 2005), students could write *citadel* for C and *yoga* for Y. As it may be harder to find relevant words for Q and Z, students can write about features that are not present; that is, Q could be *no queens* and Z might be *no zebras*. For X, students can use words like *eXcellent* or *eXpert to* describe a feature discussed in the text, such as *excellent mud bricks*. This task can be started in class and finished for homework or be done completely in class.

3. Once the handout is completed, have students form small groups and share their responses. Tell students to select one word or phrase for each letter; if all students have the same thing, they should use that, but if they differ,

students need to discuss their responses and reach a consensus about what they will use.

4. For each word/phrase selected, tell students to write one sentence about it. They can work together for each letter or divide up the letters between them and work individually. In an alphabet book about the Indus River civilization, a sentence for C could be *A citadel looked down on the city from a hill and protected the people.* For Q, a sentence could be *Maybe they had queens but archeologists don't really know what kind of government they had.*

5. After the first draft is written, tell students to work in their groups to peer edit, revise, and then write a final copy of their ABC books.

6. Assess the ABC books according to a checklist that you and students jointly devise (see the Appendix for a sample checklist).

7. When the ABC books are completed, photocopy them so students have a copy of every book created. Students can then use them as study guides for tests.

CAVEATS AND OPTIONS

1. If students individually write sentences in Step 4, they will probably need more time to complete this task than if they worked together.

2. Instead of waiting until a chapter is finished, students fill out the handout while they are reading it.

3. Students work in small groups to determine the words or phrases for each letter instead of doing it first by themselves.

4. Students spend a few class periods working exclusively on this activity instead of spreading it out over several periods.

5. Given more time, students write compositions about the academic topic instead of isolated sentences.

6. Students illustrate their ABC books by drawing pictures or finding images on the Internet.

7. Students publish their ABC books on a class wiki, and each group comments on the other groups' books.

REFERENCES AND FURTHER READING

Langston, L. (2005). *Explore the ancient world* (2nd ed.). Brea, CA: Ballard & Tighe.

VI

APPENDIX: *Sample Assessment Checklist*

Checklist for an ABC book

_____ Information makes sense (10 points)

_____ Information is in alphabetical order (15 points)

_____ All 26 letters are included (10 points)

_____ At least three transitions are used; up to five are allowed (10 points)

_____ All facts are correct (15 points)

_____ Group members demonstrate teamwork and cooperation (10 points)

_____ Groups stay on task (10 points)

_____ Book is creative and colorful (5 points)

_____ Language usage is correct: grammar, spelling, capitalization, punctuation (10 points)

_____ Book is neatly written (5 points)

Total Points _____ Letter Grade _____

Comments:

How Terms Are Used

Gordon West

Levels	*Intermediate to advanced*
Aims	*Practice looking at vocabulary that may give clues as to the political leanings of the publication*
	Understand how different terminology is produced and used
	Develop critical evaluation skills in reading
Class Time	*30–45 minutes*
Preparation Time	*15 minutes*
Resources	*Printouts of a news story on the same topic from three or four newspapers*

PROCEDURE

1. Find a large (inter)national news story that is discussed in three or four newspapers with different perspectives and different editorial stances on the issue. Papers accessible online and even reputable blogs, which students can access to search for themselves, are preferable. Number the articles, but keep the publication and author information intact. Try to get them to fit on one double-sided page so as not to overwhelm students with too much information. The key is to focus on the specific vocabulary used to describe the issue. If you are in the United States, one example might be a story about immigration. Try to find papers that use different terms for describing immigrants (e.g., *illegal aliens* vs. *undocumented immigrants*).

   Articles about contentious or controversial issues from different perspectives often use different lexical items with slightly different positive or negative connotations to discuss the issues depending on their stance toward the issue. For example, *illegal aliens* carries a more negative connotation than *undocumented immigrants*. While you will need some insider knowledge to find these semantic gaps, they should become apparent when reading different news sources.

VI

2. In class, put on the white board a visual scale (continuum) of political affiliation. Elicit from students examples of different political groups/leaders to put on the scale.

Left ------------------ X ------------------ Center ------------------ X ------------------ Right

Liberal/Progressive   Conservative

　　　Democratic Party   Republican Party

Above is an example again from the United States (and one that maybe not everyone would even agree with!). Although each country's politics would not necessarily line up the same way, most political parties and movements can be placed somewhere on the continuum. A conservative political stance in the United States is very different from a conservative political stance in Korea, for example. This is not a perfect representation, but a rough approximation. Try to present it without bias toward one political leaning or the other. Explain that newspapers and even individual writers also often have a place on this continuum.

3. Have students determine the topic of the articles, and then have them look for the main idea of each article. Try to draw out differences if there are any. Discuss the content.

4. Have students read the articles again, this time looking for differences in terms. Have them write the different terms used to refer to the same item on the board. Ask them to discuss the different terms. What are the feelings that they associate with each term? Is there one that they prefer over the other? Why? Where would they put the terms on the political continuum?

5. Discuss where the terms actually fit on the political continuum and what that can tell us about the political leanings of the publication. Some are difficult to place because they are roughly in the middle, but most will probably have a left or right leaning.

6. After doing this activity, have students follow up by keeping track of "political" words in their vocabulary journals, logs, or word cards. Have students share what they have found later as a follow-up.

CAVEATS AND OPTIONS

1. This activity does not have to be done only with a news story as it is represented across national or regional press. You can have students analyze texts from different international sources that cover the same story, but this will also introduce different lexical issues across those different sources. Words may not have the same connotations in the U.S. press as they would in

a newspaper from Ghana, for example. It is important to be aware of the increased complexity of analysis in this context, both lexically and politically.

2. Another option is for students in an EFL or business English setting who might need to communicate in the future with others using English as a lingua franca. They could compare news stories and vocabulary in those stories from different countries to see variations in use across Englishes.

3. In academic English courses, students can read texts from several different sources about the same topic (i.e., tourism, not necessarily just one story) to analyze the different words that are used across texts in that subject.

VI

Poster Carousels

Averil Coxhead

Levels	**Any**
Aims	**Encounter target lexical items in reading, writing, listening, and speaking**
	Repeat target lexical items in meaning-focused speaking and writing
Class Time	**1–3 hours**
Preparation Time	**5 minutes**

I first heard about this idea through reading Lynch and McLean's (2000) article on task repetition for language learning in class. Students select their own resources for this activity. I have used this activity with postgraduate English for academic purposes students who brought to class academic journal articles in their specialist subject. I have also used it with business and architecture classes in Hungary and with native and nonnative speakers in master's classes in applied linguistics.

PROCEDURE

1. Explain to the class that they will be preparing and presenting a poster for a class mini-conference. For their poster, they need to select a text that they would normally read as part of their study or job, related to their English for specific purposes context. Check that they know what a poster presentation for a conference is, or have an example handy to show the class if you can.

2. Discuss with the class the kind of reading they might select for preparing their poster, for example, journal articles, book chapters, magazine articles from specialist publications. Ask students to bring some articles in to the next class.

3. In the next class, put students in small groups and ask them to introduce the articles to the group (briefly), with the aim of selecting one that they will use for their poster presentation. Discussing their articles with classmates allows students to explain their choices and gauge which articles will be the most interesting. Ask students to identify vocabulary in the article that is important to the topic.

4. Once everyone has an article to present, ask them to mock up an A3 size poster (on computer or freehand) using graphics and text. The poster should contain the main ideas of the article as well as a section on why this article is important to the presenter. Ask students to ensure that key vocabulary from their article is presented on the poster as part of the text.

5. Make sure all students have a chance to run their drafts of their posters past you or a classmate to get some feedback on ideas and presentation.

6. Once the posters are complete, set up the mini-conference. You can set up the room with half the posters on the walls and the presenters standing by their posters. Have everyone else in the room become delegates at the conference, and ask them to select at least three poster presentations that they would like to hear and ask questions about. Ask the presenters to talk to their classmates/delegates and answer any questions. Give the speakers the task of using the target vocabulary from the poster in their presentations at least twice and explaining any technical meanings if necessary.

7. Once everyone has presented his or her poster several times and the delegates have listened to at least three presentations, ask the delegates to put up their own posters to present and ask the presenters from the first round to now become the delegates. Repeat the rounds of presentations and discussions.

8. Once the second round is finished, ask everyone to reflect on the presentations and posters. What would they do differently and why? What would they keep the same and why? What target vocabulary from this activity is important for their jobs/study, and how will they endeavor to maintain these words in their vocabulary?

CAVEATS AND OPTIONS

1. Keep the posters on display with a copy of the original articles so students can read the posters and the articles in their own time outside class once the activity is over.

2. Invite other classes or teachers to come along to the mini-conference to hear the presentations.

3. Have the presenters prepare a PowerPoint presentation (or similar) and present their article to the class one by one, as a regular paper in a conference would be presented.

REFERENCES AND FURTHER READING

Lynch, T., & McLean, J. (2000). Exploring the benefits of task repetition and recycling for classroom language learning. *Language Teaching Research, 4,* 221–250. doi:10.1177/136216880000400303

Content-Based Lessons: Academic Writing

Mary Martha Savage

Levels	*Intermediate to advanced*
Aims	*Use content vocabulary and cohesive strategies in writing responses*
	Use academic language to express ideas
Class Time	*15–30 minutes*
Preparation Time	*15 minutes*
Resources	*Two large pieces of chart paper*
	Handout on lined paper (Appendix A)
	Grading rubric (Appendix B)

PROCEDURE

1. Select a proverb for discussion, for example:

   When you lie with dogs, you will rise up with fleas. (Shortened title: Dogs/Fleas)

   When a door closes, a window opens. (Shortened title: Door/Window)

   Measure three times, stitch once. (Shortened title: Measure/Stitch)

2. Display the proverb in written form on PowerPoint or on the overhead projector.

3. Let students read it silently and discuss in pairs what it means. Walk around class and engage in the conversations. Help with vocabulary. Capture key vocabulary, as you hear it, on a large piece of chart paper attached to the wall. Write a shortened title of the proverb at the top of the chart. Offer additional words in conversations with students. The vocabulary could be related directly to the proverb or represent academic language used to express ideas (e.g., *this shows that, in a similar way*).

4. Lead a whole-class discussion on the literal and figurative meaning of the proverb. Capture key vocabulary during discussion, and add it to the proverb

VI

chart. Ask students to explain any words on the chart that others might not know. Offer alternative vocabulary for ideas described in less than academic ways (student: *He made a difference;* teacher: *He was a catalyst?*).

5. Have students return to pair work to discuss possible applications of the proverb for life. Encourage students to give specific examples. Capture key expressions that introduce application examples. Record them on another piece of large chart paper titled Linking Vocabulary.

Examples for beginning level:

> *For example*
>
> *Further*
>
> *In addition*

Advanced examples:

> *This proverb illustrates*
>
> *The fleas represent*
>
> *An example that would show this is*
>
> *Let me illustrate with an example from*
>
> *From this example it is clear that*

6. Review the information on the chart paper with the whole class. Have students work in pairs to review the proverb, its meaning, and its link to everyday life. Encourage use of chart vocabulary and linking expressions.

7. Use the grading rubric in Appendix B as a guide for students as they write. Have them use these labels: literal and figurative meaning, explanation, example, and application.

8. Walk around the class and offer one-to-one guidance and feedback.

CAVEATS AND OPTIONS

1. This approach will be new for some cultures where active discussion is not part of the learning process. Listening to classmates' comments and noticing words going up on chart paper may not come naturally. Instruction and assessment benefits from explicit connection from you with grading and participation so that students will engage with the idea of using the chart paper for individualized writing.

2. Keep the chart paper up on the walls for future points of student reference. Use it in future lessons as a review for academic writing and thinking. Highlight vocabulary on writing that reflects "chart use."

3. Ask students to contribute proverbs from their countries.

4. Move from proverbs to short readings, quotes, or YouTube videos.

REFERENCES AND FURTHER READING

Graves, M., & Watts-Taffe, S. (2002). The place of word consciousness in a research-based vocabulary program. In A. Farstrup & J. Samuels (Eds.), *What research has to say about reading instruction* (pp. 140–158). Newark, DE: International Reading Association.

Scott, J., Jamieson-Noel, D., & Asselin, M. (2003). Vocabulary instruction throughout the day in twenty-three Canadian upper elementary classrooms. *Elementary School Journal, 103*, 269–286.

Stahl, S., & Nagy, W. (2006). *Teaching word consciousness.* Mahwah, NJ: Lawrence Erlbaum.

APPENDIX A: *Handout for Proverb*

Name _____

When you lie down with dogs, you rise with fleas.

VI

Directions: Explain the literal and figurative meaning of this proverb. Give an example and application to life. Use strong vocabulary and cohesive language.

Content Language

Linking Language

APPENDIX B: *Rubric for In-Class Writing*

Name _____

Score _____/40 pts

First draft

Proverb: When you lie down with dogs, you rise up with fleas.

Content	/10 pts

- Explained literal meaning

- Explained figurative meaning

- Gave a specific life application

Organization	/10 pts

- First sentence explained the basic meaning

- Transitions

- Academic language for linking

Academic Language	/10 pts

- Used words off the charts

- Used academic language to express ideas

- Used correct and appropriate strings of words

Intelligibility	/5 pts

- All sentences were understandable
- Grammar was at a level appropriate for accuracy

Mechanics	/5 pts

- Spelling on common words
- Punctuation

Comments